Praise for

THE RETAIL LEADER'S ROADMAP

"This book takes you to the retail gym to discover and unleash the retail athlete within. Fully realizing your potential requires working from the inside out. Embrace the ownership and discipline required and be prepared to realize the rewards."

—**STEVE STICKEL**, former EVP of Global Stores and Operations, Old Navy

"Brian always stood out to me because of his centeredness. He draws strength from an internal compass that has guided him throughout his accomplished career. As a lifelong learner and positive thinker, his energy is contagious and inspires others to follow."

—**SONIA SYNGAL**, former CEO of Old Navy and Gap Inc

"Brian's valuable insights and strategies will undoubtedly empower leaders to cultivate a culture of engagement, leading to strong outcomes for both individuals and organizations."

—**NANCY GREEN**, former CEO and President of Old Navy

"As a field that often attracts accidental careers, we need authentic, empathetic, and experienced voices that can offer a robust framework for success. The Retail Leader's Roadmap provides precisely that, and will undoubtedly be one of the most talked-about books in the industry for years to come."

—**RON THURSTON**, Co-Founder of Ossy, podcast host, and bestselling author of *Retail Pride*

"Brian possesses a profound understanding of how effective leadership impacts teams and organizations. He is an expert in engaging employees to nurture engagement and drive exceptional results."

—**CHAD KESSLER**, EVP of Vertical Brands and Dick's Sporting Goods

"What truly sets Brian apart and makes him exceptional is his capacity to lead with empathy, a consistently positive outlook, and a profound commitment to mutual respect. Such leadership qualities are a rarity, particularly in the fast-paced and competitive realm of retail."

—**BOBBY GOODWIN**, VP, DTC Merchandising for VANS Americas

"Brian's search for inspiration and relentless ideation is as much to motivate his teams as it is to satisfy his own boundless curiosity. If you take away even a fraction as much from this book as I have from Brian's leadership and support, it will be a wonderful investment of your time."

"One determined man working hard will never impact an organization in the way one person generating enthusiasm in others to get the work done cohesively always will. Brian has grown from the man who "does" into a man who "shares". That journey is compelling and inspiring to all who join it."

"In my 10 years of working with him, Brian Librach has shown himself as a natural coach, leader, and supporter, always in service to others. He embodies all of the best leadership attributes: authenticity, humility, empowerment and cheerleading. As a coach, he brings out the best in others; as a co-worker, he is the one you want to draft first for your team. Brian can help you unlock the best you have to offer and provide a roadmap to your success."

THE RETAIL LEADER'S ROADMAP

**TAKE CONTROL OF YOUR CAREER,
UNLOCK YOUR POTENTIAL,
AND DRIVE TOWARD
RETAIL LEADERSHIP SUCCESS**

BRIAN LIBRACH

WINDERMERE
PRESS

THE RETAIL LEADER'S ROADMAP
Take Control of Your Career, Unlock Your Potential,
and Drive Toward Retail Leadership Success
First Edition

ISBN   978-1-962341-28-8   *Hardcover*
           978-1-962341-27-1   *Paperback*
           978-1-962341-30-1   *Ebook*

I dedicate this book to the countless individuals whose influence and support have shaped the path that led me to where I stand today. This book serves as a guide on seizing control of your own career, emphasizing independence while acknowledging the invaluable impact of those who have shared their wisdom and encouragement.

Foremost, my heartfelt dedication goes to my parents, my mother, and father. My early years were defined by the unwavering support of my mother, who, despite battling extreme anxiety, ensured my attendance at baseball practice, even when my father was committed to his own work. My father's unconventional parenting methods left a lasting imprint on my character, reflecting in my roles as an adult, husband, father, employee, leader, and co-worker. His lessons, such as teaching me about consequences, molded my understanding of responsibility. Living with my idol under the same roof proved a privilege that set the standard for my aspirations.

Throughout my career, I had the privilege of working under exceptional leaders who recognized my potential and pushed me to surpass my limits. These mentors were instrumental in my growth, challenging me to deliver my very best and guiding me through the intricacies of hard work. To those leaders, too numerous to list, I express my deepest gratitude.

To the individuals who, on paper, reported to me but, in reality, taught me the true meaning of leadership—you were the motivation that fueled my enthusiasm every morning. Without your commitment, there would be no version of me that exists today.

Last, but most imortantly! My profound appreciation extends to my incredible wife, Mellissa, and our son, Jax.

Mellissa, my partner in every adventure, has weathered the storms and celebrated the triumphs by my side. From enduring the loss of a child to navigating through job changes and relocations, she has been my anchor. Mellissa, a business owner, author, and fitness and executive coach, consistently challenges me to bring my best self to our home, mirroring the dedication demanded in the professional realm. She has been my compass, providing direction and purpose without which I'd be lost.

Jax, my son and constant reminder of the ongoing journey of learning, brings immeasurable joy and inspiration. Fatherhood, undoubtedly the most challenging role I've assumed, is a responsibility I hold with unwavering dedication. Jax, with his unique blend of tenacity and kindness, serves as a beacon of inspiration, raising the bar for what it means to be a man and a father. His limitless potential fuels my commitment to set an example worthy of emulation.

This book is dedicated to all these remarkable individuals who have shaped my journey, and I am profoundly grateful for the impact each of you has had on my life.

CONTENTS

Introduction   1

PILLAR 1. BUILD YOUR CHARACTER   13

One. Outwork   15

Two. Outlearn   21

Three. Be the Example   33

Four. Be Accountable   47

Five. Be Disciplined   65

PILLAR 2. BUILD YOUR CONNECTIONS   77

Six. Development   79

Seven. Communication   107

Eight. Influence   127

PILLAR 3. BUILD YOUR PLAN   147

Nine. Earn While You Learn 149

Ten. Retail University   183

Conclusion   221

About the Author   229

THE RETAIL LEADER'S ROADMAP

**TAKE CONTROL OF YOUR CAREER,
UNLOCK YOUR POTENTIAL,
AND DRIVE TOWARD
RETAIL LEADERSHIP
➡ SUCCESS ⬅**

BRIAN LIBRACH

YEARS OR AGE ALONE WON'T CAUSE YOUR CAREER TO DIE. NOT HAVING A PLAN, A LACK OF CHARACTER, AND A LACK OF CONNECTIONS WILL DO YOU IN MUCH SOONER.

INTRODUCTION

I didn't know it at the time, but growing up with ADHD in an era where most folks didn't know what it was, much less how to work with it, was one of the best lessons of my life.

I remember in elementary school, the principal and my teacher called my folks into school one day to suggest they put me on Ritalin. I am guessing I was a handful. My father told them without hesitation, "No, his grades are fine, and you need to find a way to keep up with his energy."

Nobody taught me how to cope with my lack of executive functioning skills. I learned through trial and error. I benefited from the drivenness that comes from having ADHD and, luckily for me, found healthy ways to chase the dopamine. And luckily, although my brain doesn't make dopamine like non-ADH-Ders, it *definitely* responds to endorphins the same way, so I chase those too. When I was young, it was baseball and fitness, and as I grew up, it became retail and a strong desire to beat my dad to each milestone he had reached in his career at an earlier age than he had been able to. Along the way, tattoos and motorcycles crept in as my therapy. Building a career in retail leadership, I had to continually find ways to motivate and drive myself when my brain often wanted to keep me parked in place, and making sure I'm getting a steady flood of endorphins means I love playing the game just as much as I love winning.

It wasn't until I was 21 years old and tasked with leading as a district manager for the first time in Scottsdale, Arizona, that I learned how to articulate how I was coping. Prior to reading the book "The Tao of Personal Leadership" by Diane Dreher, I just reacted to things as they occurred. This book helped put into words what I was doing all along. The art of Yin and Yang. I always paid attention to my health from a body standpoint. This was the beginning of my understanding and applying the mind and soul parts of health.

Basically, I taught myself how to get unstuck. Every time I faced that feeling of not being where I wanted to be, I pushed through using any wisdom I could get my hands on at the time.

It would have been a lot easier, and faster, if I'd had a guide like this book. So, I wrote it myself.

In my years of experience, I've noticed that when retail leaders, whether early or late in their careers, face challenges, it often traces back to a key area of success. For instance, a leader at the peak of their career might struggle to motivate one person, a few people, or a team at a certain time. They might need to re-focus, recognize a skill gap, or face a challenge that looks different in their current role or under new circumstances. What "outworking" means for a store manager can be very different from a district manager's perspective. Likewise, successful communication may vary from one company to another, requiring adaptation and learning.

Google says the average vehicle has only an 11.8% chance of making it to 250,000 miles. It makes me wonder 1) what these cars have that 88.2% of cars don't, 2) why 250,000 miles is the benchmark with today's technology, and 3) where they get this data from because I sure don't see many vehicles with this many miles on the road.

Mileage alone won't cause your car to die. Accidents, neglected maintenance, deferred repairs, rust, repeated contact with potholes, and weather can accelerate wear and tear.

So, what does this all have to do with retail leadership? Retailers aren't much different from mechanics. We both need to be good at vocational skills. Both mechanics and retail leaders need to be fit for the physical and mental work that sits in front of them every single day.

What's different is mechanics take care of vehicles, and retail leaders take care of people. You can argue it's okay if a vehicle only lasts for 250,000 miles. This is not okay when you talk about people. Folks likely will work from 16 to 65, so let's round up to 50 years, and I think we can all agree that's a lot more mileage than 250,000.

Years or age alone won't cause your career to die. Not

having a plan, a lack of character, and a lack of connections will do you in much sooner.

In this book, you will learn a complete roadmap to retail leadership success. I don't believe I have all the answers, but I do believe I have a series of answers that will help you get unstuck and find your rhythm.

THE NON-TRADITIONAL PATH

You will need more than a traditional education to succeed at any retail leadership level. Notice how I mentioned the word "succeed", not "start"—a traditional education can definitely help you get your foot in the door (and my theory is that this is because most people who spent hundreds of thousands of dollars and anywhere from 4 to 8 years of their life on a traditional education need a reason to look down on those who didn't). But a traditional education isn't the ticket to retail leadership success.

My non-diagnosed ADHD, lack-of-executive-functioning ass didn't spend a single day in college. Ok, that's a lie—I spent a single hour at Orange Coast Community College, which I initially enrolled in because it was ranked a top 10 party college. It only took an hour there for me to ask for a refund.

Nowadays, I have the incredible good fortune of being married to an executive coach and wellness business owner. My wife, Mellissa, gives me the kind of coaching top corporate execs pay thousands of dollars a year for. I'm so grateful to have that—my brain needs the executive help. When I look at my son, I'm looking in the mirror, and I'm reminded of so much of what I was going through as a kid with ADHD who didn't fit the traditional school mold. I've found in my career that so many others in retail share this trait. Maybe it's because ADHD gives us the superpowers of improvisation, people skills, quick problem solving, and not being freaked out by change. It's almost like we were born for it.

A traditional education absolutely can help you if you outworked and outlearned folks when you attended it. With or without a traditional education, however, you will need to educate yourself regularly throughout your entire career. You will need to understand what is required of the next role at all times by staying attentive and you will need to seek out the education on your own. You will also need to pay attention to what it takes to keep your own role with the constant change that occurs at all levels.

If you don't know your destination, you can end up moving aimlessly through life and end up wherever you end up. If you want to end up where you want to, you have to have a general idea of its location and work backwards from the destination to ensure you take the right roads and in the appropriate amount of time. You must create realistic and unrealistic goals and work backwards from both. More often than not, once you get some momentum going, you will find yourself achieving most goals somewhere in the middle of both timeframes.

I wrote this book to help people get unstuck. To help people like yourself that are interested in growing yourself and in return growing those you are leading or even being led by. The steps in this book are not theoretical; they are real-life lessons that I am sharing with you because they have worked over and over again for myself and for thousands of people I have been privileged enough to work with and alongside.

WHY THE HELL SHOULD YOU LISTEN TO ME?

I am retail. It's my blood. Literally. Look up my last name on google and you will see merchants and manufacturing dating back to the 1800s in Poland. My grandfather owned a retail store in Springfield, Missouri and my Pops was a Vice President of Planning and Allocation back in the 80's and 90's.

As soon as I was old enough to sit at the dining room table, I was listening and learning about retail. Most people refer to retail as an accidental career, I chose retail (after I realized a professional baseball career wasn't in the cards).

In my career, I've been up, way up. I've been down, way down. I've been written up for making long distance phone calls from the sales floor for hours. I've said I couldn't work

Sundays because football is on TV. I've had a district manager have to call and wake me up when I was supposed to be at a meeting because I partied too much the night before. I was fired for "performance" when I was 30 and had another role "eliminated" when I was 38 (and again when I was 48) for budgetary reasons.

But I also progressed from the stockroom to the corner office with 3 years of High School and no college. I was a District Manager at 21, Regional Director at 25, Director of Stores at 35 and VP of Stores at 38.

I've frequented biker bars. I have spent thousands of hours in a tattoo parlor having therapy for my perceived trauma. Felt more appropriate for me than a shrink's couch. It doesn't hurt when you become great friends with the owners of multiple shops. I've moved over 30 times, ran stores, districts and regions out of New York, Florida, California, Arizona, Chicago, Cleveland and Canada as well as two different stints running all stores in North America. I've owned 8 homes, 3 motorcycles, 10+ Ford F 150's, and sat at the corner office twice. None of these things have filled up my cup and satisfied me in any way. It's always been, what's next? What don't I have?

The only time I have truly found fulfillment is when I see my impact on someone's growth. So that's why I wrote this book: my goal is to pass on my hard-earned wisdom to the next generation of retail leaders, and to positively impact as many

THE RETAIL LEADER'S ROADMAP

people as possible.

THE RETAIL LEADER'S ROADMAP

If you're feeling stuck or have hit a plateau in your career, this book is for you.

Imagine you're a General Manager who has been in the role for 6–7 years. You see others advancing to District Manager and wonder, "What am I missing? What more can I do?" You're searching for that push, that insight that will elevate you to the next level.

This book is your guide to unlocking the next phase of your retail leadership journey. It will help you build a plan to achieve retail leadership success within 3–5 years. We'll explore the critical practices to get you unstuck and propel you upward in your career. These practices include identifying areas where you might be faltering, diagnosing the root causes, and understanding the structure of successful retail management.

The beauty of retail is that you get out what you put in. This book will teach you exactly what to put in and how to do it, putting you in complete control of your career outcomes.

You can choose to read this book cover to cover, which I recommend doing the first time you read it. From there, I recommend you keep this book close to you so you can reference this book when you find yourself stuck and simply read the particular chapter in need.

Here's a quick guide for how each retail leadership should approach this book.

SALES ASSOCIATES, STORE SUPPORT LEADERS, AND INDIVIDUAL CONTRIBUTORS

Focus on Parts I and III. The hard skills are crucial for you to acquire and excel in, as they are the vocational skills associated with your role. A roadmap will also be vital as you plan your path to the next level or role.

STORE AND GENERAL MANAGERS, AND STORE DIRECTORS

Read the entire book first, study each part, highlight, and make notes. Then, revisit areas where you see the greatest opportunity for growth.

DISTRICT LEADERS

Read the book cover to cover twice. On your first read, focus on identifying your blind spots or skill set deficiencies. On the second read, focus on these aspects within your team's performance. Make notes next to sections for coaching individuals who work for you.

REGIONAL AND SENIOR MANAGER LEVEL LEADERS

Every part of this book offers benefits. Your focus should depend on where you or your team members are stuck. If you or someone you are considering has been in the same job for over four years, start with Part III. If there's a loss of motivation and a tendency towards negativity, focus on Part I. If there's consistent high performance but a struggle to advance, lean into Part II.

DIRECTORS AND VICE PRESIDENTS

Directly proceed to the sections on influence, particularly focusing on Ego and Emotion. Consider how your identity has been shaped by your career progress and how emotions play a larger role at your level. Reflect on how often you find yourself defending your self-image, whether to family, employees, or superiors.

CHIEF OFFICERS, INCLUDING THE CEO

Before making drastic changes in your team, assess whether the issues lie with you or others. As a top leader, you're likely to exhibit stronger selfish tendencies, a larger ego, and more intense emotions. Read Part II for self-awareness and the longevity of your organization. Once you've gained insight, read the rest to ensure your team embodies great leadership qualities.

BOARD MEMBERS

Your expertise and background make you a crucial part of the organization. Reading this book will help ensure the CEO's selfish tendencies are constructive, their ego is being used for good instead of being avoided as a bad word, and emotions don't hinder decision-making. Part II, focusing on selfishness, ego, and emotions, is particularly relevant for you.

WALK WITH ME

Everyone should keep this book nearby and go back to it each and every time you find yourself or someone you are accountable to stuck and not getting the results or promotions you want.

This book is about making and acting in a way that increases your odds of success. Nothing is 100%, but if you lean into these practices you will win much more often than not.

I believe you can become best in class in any role or responsibility you have in the retail store environment in 3 to 5 years just like a university education. I am going to bet this also expands outside of retail, but I'm going to stick in my lane.

You too can become the best DM, RD, or Vice President on your team or a leader in your field if you can successfully navigate the first 8 practices we'll touch on in this book. You can position yourself to take on additional roles and responsibilities and win right out of the gate in this new role or responsibility if you master the last 3 practices.

Before you begin Pillar One, I want to ask that you pick a song that really rallies you. If you were walking (or strutting, or swaggering) on stage or out from the locker room to the court, what music do you want playing in the background? Play that song for yourself now, and pump yourself up. This especially goes for my fellow ADHDers—music creates a huge dopamine release. It can shift your mood, energize your body, and empower your mind, making you feel more confident and ready to tackle challenges. So play that favorite pump-up anthem a few times before you turn the page and begin this journey.

Ready? Walk with me.

BUILD YOUR CHARACTER

THE HARD SKILLS ARE YOUR PREREQUISITE FOR EVERYTHING YOU GET TO DO AS A LEADER. THIS IS WHERE YOU EARN THE RESPECT OF OTHERS AND BUILD THE CONFIDENCE REQUIRED OF BEING A LEADER. THESE ARE THE VOCATIONAL SKILLS REQUIRED TO BECOME PROFICIENT AT YOUR CRAFT.

YOUR MIND AND HEART TAKE WHAT YOU SAY AND THINK SERIOUSLY.

CHAPTER ONE

OUTWORK

"Never let anyone outwork you."

This is the first thing I can ever remember learning from my dad. He would say to me, "Hard work is the only thing within your control. So if you outwork everyone, you will always be in a position to win."

Based on the past 30+ years of my career in retail, I can say with confidence that Dad was right.

Let me kick off this discussion of the first practice in the Retail Leader's Roadmap, Outwork, with some myth-busting. "Work smarter, not harder" only gets you so far. In fact, I call bullshit on the whole saying. You get to work smarter when you have earned the right to do so through hard work. And by the time you're working smarter, you're ready for more, so you can take on more work. So you should think of it as both. Work smarter and harder.

When I was in my fourth year as a district manager, I

remember working for someone who really pushed the smarter versus harder thing. I learned a ton during this time, how to leverage my time and communication to get more accomplished as just a couple of examples. Interestingly though, I found myself working harder at learning how to do these things. So my hard work simply shifted from the obvious rolling up of my sleeves to the less obvious learning agility.

This was my last year as District Manager before taking on a Regional Director role and it made sense that I was able to redirect my attention to working smarter, because I had built a strong foundation already by working harder. It was, however, exhausting work learning how to leverage things more effectively—how to spend 2 hours preparing for a conversation that would take 15 minutes to have in order to get exactly what I needed from the conversation. But I did it, because my dad's voice rang in my head. Never let anyone outwork you.

Your career isn't a marathon. It's a series of sprints. Each sprint should leave you gassed. If you have gas left in the tank at the end of the day, you left something on the table.

LEADERS EAT LAST

The Outwork practice is a key part of your leadership, and so many leaders miss this; they're looking for their team to work hard, instead of themselves. They think they're done outworking everyone. Not the case.

First one in and last one out. Early on in any new relationship when you are building your character, you will need to show that you are willing to work harder and do more than anyone else. This is where showing up before anyone and never leaving before anyone comes into play.

As Simon Sinek writes in Leaders Eat Last:

The true price of leadership is the willingness to place the needs of others above your own. Great leaders truly care about those they are privileged to lead and understand that the true cost of the leadership privilege comes at the expense of self-interest.

Back when I was a store manager, I was opening a new Outlet store in Ontario Mills, California. I'll never forget my first day there. I showed up early, all pumped up and ready to go, only to find my Regional Director and a bunch of sales associates already waiting for me at the mall gate. I was five minutes ahead of schedule, but before I could even say 'Hi' to anyone, my Regional Director pulled me aside and just went off on me. He was fuming about how I should never arrive after my team and what kind of example that set. There were lots of swear words. It was a different time.

Fast forward a few years: same Regional Director, but this time around, I was a District Manager, working directly under him. We were on our first store tour together, heading into the

Fiesta Mall in Arizona. Back then, it was one of the company's top-performing stores.

As soon as we walked in, I greeted the store manager and headed to the backroom to drop off my laptop bag and grab a quick sip of coffee. But just like at Ontario Mills, I barely had a moment before getting yanked aside for a stern talking-to. My boss was livid, questioning why I started off in the backroom and what kind of example I was setting. He made it clear that my priorities were all wrong.

That experience changed how I approached store visits for years. From then on, I'd leave my laptop bag behind the cash wrap and stay away from the backroom for the first hour or two. It made a huge difference. The teams knew I was there for them, and that being visible and present on the sales floor was what mattered most. I'd do my computer work right out on the floor, using a folding cart, so I could stay engaged with the team.

I also started giving the store teams a heads-up about any backroom work I absolutely had to do. I'd let them know when I'd be back there, how long it'd take, and why it was necessary. This helped a lot in managing perceptions and showing where my focus really was.

I took one thing he said with me: Stay out of the backroom and get off your ass! That's a good mantra to start with when you're building the Outwork pillar.

THE FRONT LINE COMES FIRST

"Your employees come first. And if you treat your employees right, guess what? Your customers come back, and that makes your shareholders happy. Start with employees and the rest follows from that."

This comment from the co-founder and CEO of Southwest Airlines, Herb Kelleher resonated with me early on in my leadership career, and I've brought it along with me all these years. It gave me and should give you permission to have empathy for our employees and to make our employees our #1 customer.

Multi-Store leaders are the face of the brand to the largest population of employees. Your store employees see the District and Regional Managers as representation of the corporate or home office.

Most VPs and above spend the majority of their time in meetings and on calls. They tend to be working more behind the scenes on strategy and cross organizationally to help ensure the customer experience is seamless. So, the productivity of the organization lives and dies in the hands of the front line workers and the leaders that develop and inspire them. Of course, the product needs to be great—but if the front line workers and field leadership misrepresent that product, you are dead in the water.

You can always tell where leadership is breaking down by

the way the front line is holding up. I travel a lot for work and therefore have had the opportunity to shop hundreds of different Starbucks locations. I also lived at one point in time in Venice Beach, California, and had multiple Starbucks to choose from within a couple of miles.

The Starbucks I regularly went to was one in Santa Monica that was fantastic. But I would avoid the other ones in the area because the experience was not the best. This is a sign of a great store leader—but not a good district manager. On the flip side, I've been to areas where I can frequent 5 to 6 different Starbucks within a couple miles of each other and have the same great experience in all of them. This is the sign of a great district manager.

Remember that the example and inspiration you set is what your front line will look like. So bring a culture of Outwork. Make that your calling card among the people you lead. Let them know that you will always outwork for them, and in turn, they'll outwork for the company.

CHAPTER TWO

OUTLEARN

Once, a long time ago, there was a wise Zen master. People from far and near would seek his counsel and ask for his wisdom. Many would come and ask him to teach them, enlighten them in the way of Zen. He seldom turned any away.

One day an important man, a man used to command and obedience came to visit the master. "I have come today to ask you to teach me about Zen. Open my mind to enlightenment." The tone of the important man's voice was one used to getting his own way.

The Zen master smiled and said that they should discuss the matter over a cup of tea. When the tea was served the master poured his visitor a cup. He poured and he poured and the tea rose to the rim and began to spill over the table and finally onto the robes of the wealthy man. Finally the visitor shouted, "Enough. You are spilling the tea all over. Can't you see the cup is full?"

The master stopped pouring and smiled at his guest. "You

are like this tea cup, so full that nothing more can be added. Come back to me when the cup is empty. Come back to me with an empty mind.

If you think you know everything, someone who doesn't will find the better answer.

Learning is working smarter—which will let you work harder.

Why are outworking and outlearning dependent on each other? It's all about learning agility combined with action orientation.

Practice doesn't make perfect; perfect practice does. What's the difference? Let's take golf as an example. They say if you practice your swing by adjusting the direction you hit the ball to make your slice land where you need it, you'll fail more often than not. You need to practice the swing as it's meant to be, until you can hit the ball correctly with the right technique. This shows the need to be open to learning. However, if you learn and don't apply what you've learned, then what's the point of learning at all? This is where outworking comes in. If you don't work hard, once you learn what you should be doing in practice, you won't improve.

If you want to become a leader, not just a doer, you need to learn. As doers, you might get away with not knowing how you do certain things and just be talented enough to get it done. But if you're leading others, that won't cut it. You have to be able to explain how things are done for others to learn.

Sure, some folks will learn just by the example you set, but when it's time for them to explain it to someone else, they won't be able to, and the development stops. While some can learn from examples, many need to be told how. If you don't know how, you can't tell anybody.

So, to become a leader, you'll need to be able to teach. And to teach, you need to be able to learn.

PUT IN THE REPS

Learning can and usually is more exhausting than doing anything else. When you are learning, you are putting in reps for the brain over brawn. When you put in reps to get fit, it's physically exhausting, when you put in reps to strengthen the brain it's mentally exhausting. Either one is exhausting, just in different ways. This is why working smarter is actually in my opinion working harder at the same time.

I can't remember where I heard this from but it really resonated with me. If you are not practicing, somebody else is, and when it comes time to compete they will outperform you. The same is true in our profession when it comes to learning. If you are not learning, somebody else is, and when it comes time to compete for the business or even your job, they will outperform you and take your business and your job.

Here's an example from my own career. It was 1996 or 1997 in Arizona. I was a newly promoted district manager and had inherited a rock star team. Together over two years we established ourselves as one of the very best teams in the brand at the time. This team was so good that I realized about 18 months into my tenure that I was out of shit to offer them. Just 18 months ago, I was doing the same job they were doing and while I had a lot to offer the team early on, I was empty.

This was my first real "aha" moment as a multi-store leader. What got me here, wasn't going to keep me here—and it sure wasn't going to propel me to achieve my goals. It also wasn't going to help those I was accountable to grow themselves into the leaders they were capable of being.

The internet wasn't widely used for education in the late nineties, so books were where the education was. This is when I started to pick up books in order to grow professionally. I hated school as a kid, mostly because my non-diagnosed ADHD got in the way of me being interested in learning most things. I hated reading because I was being told what to read. This time I was choosing books that interested me because they were topics I noticed I needed to strengthen myself in, in order to have more to offer my team.

What got you here won't get you there. Check your mindset: is it a growth mindset? Or is it fixed—meaning you already think you know what you need to know?

You know a lot. That's how you got to where you are. Give yourself a pat on the back for that.

Now get learning so you can get where you want to go next.

GROWTH MINDSET VS FIXED MINDSET

Imagine you're faced with a challenging task. If your immediate thought is "I can't do this, it's just too hard," you're likely operating under a fixed mindset. On the flip side, if you think, "This is tough, but let's see what I can learn from it," then you're leaning towards a growth mindset.

Growth mindset is what will allow you to Outlearn.

The growth mindset is rooted in the belief that our basic abilities can be developed and improved through dedication and hard work. There's that phrase again: hard work. See how Outwork and Outlearn go hand in hand? It's about loving the process, not just the end result—chasing the endorphins during the workout, not just enjoying the end result.

Fixed mindset is what keeps you stuck. The fixed mindset holds that our intelligence and talents are innate traits that we can't change in any meaningful way. So, to hold on to our sense of being smart and skilled, we avoid failure at all costs. This mindset keeps you paralyzed, unable to take the risks that lead to growth.

Recognize when you're thinking with a fixed mindset and

challenge those thoughts. Embrace challenges and see them as opportunities to grow. When you fail, don't run from it; instead, analyze what happened and learn from it. Praise the process, not just the talent. Focus on effort, strategy, and improvement, rather than just the end result.

It's not that people with a growth mindset are always successful—learning involves stumbling, falling, and failing. But people with a growth mindset know that their failures are just temporary setbacks on their learning journey, not a reflection of their abilities. This mindset can make all the difference in how we approach our goals and challenges.

COACHABILITY

Being coachable is a crucial part of professional growth. If I'm coachable, it means I'm either seeking advice or responding positively to feedback from my boss, which in turn makes them feel appreciated and invested in my growth. Being coachable is essential, and if you're not, it's important to find a way to become so. You need your boss and their boss to invest in you if you aim to ascend and grow in your career.

I remember a time when I had a new district manager working under me. Within her first year, she failed three audits in a row. Our policy stated that failing three audits could lead to a documentation, loss of bonus, and potential termination if another failure occurred. She was a great person but new to the role and made some mistakes. Her third failure was marginal. I had to talk to her about the possibility of being fired if she failed again. It was a conversation I dreaded.

But she was coachable. She put together a fail-safe plan and went after it. We aligned on what needed to be done, focusing as much on her inputs as mine. Not only did she pass her subsequent audits, but she also started scoring nearly perfect grades. We even used her strategies to teach other managers how to improve their audit performances. Her willingness to be coached and her proactive approach turned a potential failure into a learning opportunity for others.

I like to think of coachability as "learning agility". It's one thing to always be willing to learn, but it's another to actually act on that learning. I've noticed that some people nod along when I'm coaching them, and say, "That makes a lot of sense," but then they don't do anything with the information they've received. In retail, especially, you have to be able to apply what you've learned. It's not just about absorbing knowledge; it's about turning that knowledge into action and tangible results. That's where the real difference is made.

Any multi-store leader knows how great it feels when something is learned early on in a visit—and by the time the visit is over, everyone is already implementing what was learned and the work has leveled up.

BE A FEEDBACK CHAMPION

To learn, you have to be open to receiving feedback. Period.

It's a key ingredient in developing a growth mindset. You want to build a reputation for being curious—not just passively accepting feedback, but actively seeking it. The more feedback you get from others, the more they'll be interested in you. Whereas if you're closed off or seem uninterested in feedback, you'll come off as having a fixed mindset, and people will stop investing in you.

Remember, though: not all feedback is good or useful. You need to still use your brain and discern what to keep and what to respectfully reject. It's a delicate balance. Show interest in feedback and only take what makes sense.

How do you do this?

When I was 21, I read The 7 Habits of Highly Effective People by Stephen Covey, which changed my perspective. Habit 5: "Seek first to understand, then to be understood" was a game-changer. It taught me to respect those giving feedback but still to use my brain by trying things out before accepting everything as true. If something didn't work after trying it, I could explain why and propose a different approach based on my findings. Sometimes, the person giving feedback could explain their point better, and I could adjust, or I might even change their mind.

As I grew older and advanced in my career, I met people whose feedback lacked substance, leaving me to choose to look elsewhere or decipher what I was hearing. It wasn't until my early 40s that I met a boss who told me to use my brain when receiving feedback. They advised me to take time to think about it, to try it on for size and see how it fit before committing to it. They said it was just feedback based on their observations and knowledge, and it was up to me to determine its relevance. This advice became a vital part of my toolkit, and it's one of the first tools I recommend to the people I coach.

CURIOSITY WINS

"Be curious, not judgmental."

That's a great quote from Ted Lasso, which if you've never watched it, I definitely recommend giving it a look (after you finish this book, of course).

Being curious helps balance your ego. If you're curious, you believe there's something cool out there that hasn't appeared yet. Your ego typically doesn't like being uncomfortable and would rather you weren't curious. This is a coping mechanism for stepping out of your comfort zone.

Stop taking yourself so seriously. I've noticed that as people climb the leadership ladder, they start taking themselves too seriously and stop learning more than others. This happens because their ego is defending their position, and with that position often comes more demands, both personally (like financially) and professionally.

Staying constantly curious as you climb the ladder can keep you humble. It shows you and others that you're open to different viewpoints and believe something better might be out there. It encourages you to ask questions and learn from others.

If you're only curious when it obviously benefits you at a particular time, you won't be curious when you really need to be. You'll miss tremendous opportunities to learn and improve. Being curious should be a way of life, a part of your WHY. This is the only way to ensure you don't miss opportunities as they come. They say luck is the art of being in the right place at the right time. Being curious increases your chances of just that, being in the right place at the right time.

MASTER YOUR EGO, OR IT WILL BECOME YOUR GREATEST OBSTACLE

Your ego can be tricky. And most of the time, if I'm working with or coaching someone who's not progressing on the Retail Leader's Roadmap, what's standing in their way is their ego.

If you're open to learning something, it might seem like you don't know enough now—and this can trigger our ego response of feeling insecure. Sure, that's true in one sense, but you might know enough today, just not enough for tomorrow. When you think about it, it's pretty silly not to be eager to learn, because everything we know today was learned yesterday. If we hadn't learned, we wouldn't have anything to defend now.

The book I mentioned earlier, The Tao of Personal Leadership, helped me understand the importance of duality. I realized that when one person wins, someone else loses, and vice versa. This made me comfortable with the fact that I'm going to lose sometimes, and when I do win, I need to be humble enough to understand that someone else might feel bad because they lost.

What does this have to do with ego and being an obstacle to outlearning? Well, if you're afraid of losing, you tend to hold onto everything very tightly, closing yourself off to new or different ideas. You focus on proving what you already know, rather than being curious about what others might know that can improve your productivity or way of thinking.

Consider this: the best hitters in baseball miss 7 out of 10 times at the plate, and the best basketball players miss 4 to 5 out of 10 shots.

The point is, you will lose, and you'll likely lose more than you win if you keep stepping up to the plate or taking shots. However, the more you do this, the more you learn and the better you get.

When you lose, you're not a loser. Just like when you win,

you're not a winner. You just lost or won that particular battle. We can't identify with either because if we do, we'll either take ourselves too seriously or become paralyzed, never coming close to fulfilling our potential.

CHAPTER THREE

BE THE EXAMPLE

Years ago, I visited a store that had a new district manager—a pretty nerve-wracking moment for any new DM. Luckily for her, it started off great; she had one of the most beautiful stores I had seen in a long time.

On the surface, the store was exceptionally well-presented, and the team was on point. But after spending time on the floor engaging with the team, we entered the backroom, only to find over 100 cartons of what appeared to be prioritized and organized replenishment from that morning's shipment. I knew something was off.

When the district manager and team went back to the sales floor, I stayed behind. Digging through the cartons at the bottom of the stacks, I discovered new and meaningful products hidden away. The team had chosen to make the store look pretty for our visit instead of processing the most important products for the customers. The district manager, in her first year, hadn't thought to check this.

I knew this was an opportunity to set an example and shape the future of this district manager. I had a flight that night, but I chose to miss it. Why? Because after gathering the team in the backroom and showing them what I'd found, it was time to act.

I canceled my flight, booked a hotel room, rolled up my sleeves, and we all processed that meaningful product together, getting it onto the floor in time for the evening customer rush.

It was crucial for the new district manager to see action, not just hear about it. This was a chance to set a tone that would positively impact the years ahead.

The essence of being a leader isn't just about giving orders or setting rules; it's about whether people are actually following you. And how do you get people to follow you? By setting an example that's worth replicating.

By the way, this does not look like "fake it 'till you make it." In fact, I call major bullshit on that phrase. When you fake it until you make it, people see it. You think they don't know you're faking it? They'll follow suit, doing the same thing, which is unhealthy for them and everyone they interact with. It becomes a way of coping.

I remember working for someone once who was so concerned with how they were perceived by others that not only did they lead this way, but they also advertised it to anyone who worked for them, like it was a badge of honor or a technique others should master. I think this is a terrible example to set.

To grow at any level, you need to make mistakes and be encouraged to do so. Leading by "faking it" tells people they shouldn't be comfortable making mistakes or looking bad, and this will hold them back from progressing to their full capabilities.

Lead with authenticity. Lead without ego.

Think about the team captain on any sports team. They're not just the person calling the shots during the game; they're the one showing up first for practice, giving their all every time, and staying late to help pack up. This kind of dedication and commitment is infectious. It sets a standard for the rest of the team. Everyone is going to show up early, stay late, and give their all if that's what their leader is doing.

In retail leadership, with the customer-facing front line so crucial to your results, being the example for your team can literally be the difference between success and failure. How you conduct yourself sets the tone for the entire group. If you're diligent, creative, and ethical in your work, your people will likely act the same; and if you're disorganized, lazy, or won't take accountability, don't be surprised if your team reflects those traits too.

The first two practices we've gone through, Outwork and Outlearn, create the conditions for you to Be the Example. You don't have to be the smartest person in the room—and if you're doing your job right, and hiring the right people, you often won't be. Being the Example is about showing a commitment to continuous improvement and hard work. Show your team your hunger for learning and your work ethic, and watch your example create a whole new environment for them.

Not everyone is lucky enough to grow up with positive role models. I was fortunate to grow up with a father who was a role model and a hard worker, who took care of his family and was present. I realize not everyone has these privileges, so it's important for us in leadership positions to create that privilege for others. We have the opportunity to be the role models that some might not have elsewhere. This is where leaders in retail, or any field for that matter, can step in. By being a good example, they create a privilege for their employees: the privilege of having a role model to look up to and learn from. Retail, especially, is a field where "learning by doing" is paramount. Employees learn the ropes not through manuals or lectures alone, but by watching and emulating their leaders.

I vividly remember the transition from being an employee to a store manager. There was a moment when I realized all eyes were on me, and how I acted from that point forward would set an example for everyone else. I used to walk past hangers and price tags on the floor without picking them up. Then, one day, I just started picking them up. Strangely enough, I soon noticed others doing the same, without me having to tell them.

Like it or not, you are the example for your employees. And they'll follow your example whether it's a good one or a bad one—so make sure it's a great one.

THE EXAMPLE FOR YOUR PEERS

Recently, I was watching my son's basketball practice. The coach was working on fundamentals, and my son, who, like his father, tends to love doing everything with flair. I watched as he dribbled behind his back, between his legs, and finished with fancy layups. Some baskets were made, and some were not. My son just so happens to be one of the strongest 9-year-olds on the team. The rest of the team took notice of the way my son was playing. I pulled him to the side and asked him to run the drills the way the coach designed them and to do so in the very best way possible. This was to set an example for the rest of the team, both in terms of listening to the coach and understanding that fundamentals come first.

What we do day in and day out is no different. Being the captain of the team is a prerequisite for you if advancement is something you want to achieve. Your peers need to become better because of you and look to you for guidance, but more importantly, for a visual of what best in class looks like, with humility.

A key obstacle to success is not having role models. That's why being the example or the role model for everyone in your circle is so important. Don't let athletes, actors, or people they don't actually engage with be their only mentors. This is unacceptable. Role models should be people they interact with, engage with, and can learn from by actually being in their presence.

You have to be someone others aspire to be. If you're always stressed out, hate your job, or dislike your bosses, why would anyone want to take on your role? You have an obligation to make your role look appealing, fun, and rewarding. I recall a Regional Director who worked for me. One day, after flying across the country for a visit, they told me about looking out the airplane window and feeling a sense of accomplishment and appreciation. They were so grateful for the opportunities they had over the years, the places they traveled to, and the people they met. This person radiated a love for their job, and everyone around them felt it. They were intentional about it, often saying, "If what I do doesn't look enjoyable, why would anybody want to do it?"

THE EXAMPLE FOR YOUR TEAM

Eighteen months into my first district manager role, I had a bit of a wake-up call, really. I found myself running out of new things to offer my team. It was a tough spot to be in, but I knew I had to set the right example. I told them straight up that I'd hit a wall in terms of new ideas and strategies. But I didn't stop there. I knew the next step was crucial; I had to figure out what my team needed from me and learn new ways to provide that support.

This situation led me to a deeper understanding of leadership. It's not just about having all the answers or a constant stream of innovative ideas. Sometimes, it's about recognizing when you're at a standstill and being transparent about it. This moment of honesty with my team wasn't just about admitting a temporary shortfall. It was about showing them that it's okay to acknowledge your limits. And more importantly, it demonstrated the value of being willing to learn and adapt. It opened up a conversation about what they truly needed from me as their leader, which was a game-changer in how we worked together moving forward.

This goes for setting the wrong example, too. Early in my Regional Director days, I looked for two things when evaluating the character of store teams during visits with my District Managers. At the time, Pacific Sunwear had a policy that you couldn't chew gum or have drinks at the cash wrap. Whether I actually cared about these policies or not is irrelevant—they were the organization's requirements, and I used them to see how people behaved when we weren't watching. It was about integrity: doing the right thing even when no one is looking.

I would open the cash wrap drawers and often find gum sitting comfortably inside, with drinks usually placed near the printers under the registers. I used these as examples for the team.

I would ask, "Did you know this wasn't acceptable?"

They would always say yes, and I would follow up with, "If you pick and choose what rules to ignore, how can I trust you won't choose to ignore something much more important than not chewing gum or drinking behind the counter?"

I remember leaving many stores and discussing with the district manager why I questioned the integrity of a store leader who chose to chew gum or drink behind the counter when they knew they shouldn't. It might have seemed like a small thing, but I made a big deal out of it. I did this because I wanted to set an example. As multi-store leaders who seldom see our direct reports due to the number we have, we need to trust them. We also need to find ways to teach the importance of this trust to our teams.

I didn't enter my career with that kind of integrity nailed down. I had to learn how to be the example and practice it before I could teach it to others. I talked about letting go of ego in the last chapter—so, here, I'll put mine aside to show you just how bad an example I started out.

At 18, I was a Store Manager for Chess King in Cerritos, California. Honestly, I had no business handling that level of responsibility back then. So, why did I have it? Because I out-worked and outsold most others. I made money!

However, I lacked other key character traits at the time, especially the practice of being the example. I was 18, with an ID that got me into nightclubs and bars, living my best life in Southern California, and residing in Newport Beach. Close the store on a Friday? That wasn't me. Work the most important shift on a Saturday? Not if I had been out late the night before. Work on Sunday? Absolutely not; football was on TV as early as 10 am Pacific time. I would miss meetings entirely because I overslept.

Basically, I was the complete opposite of a good example.

Thankfully, a couple of years later, at 20, I ran into Dave Temple. He really shook me up and made me recognize my missteps. I was able to learn what I'm sharing with you now: that you have to walk the walk, not just talk the talk. If I wanted to succeed, I had to become someone who set an example of success. And I had to live it even when no one was watching.

(Funny side note: my father was the store manager of this exact Chess King in Cerritos, California, 20 years before me, and the store looked exactly the same—same carpet and everything!)

Act like you're in the spotlight at all times.

Imagine you're in the home office area of your company. I've been fortunate enough in my career to be a General Manager, District Manager, and Regional Director in home office markets for multiple companies. In these roles, the CEO could pop into my area of responsibility at any time. Family members might shop on weekends and share stories afterward. This kind of pressure was good for me because it kept me on my toes. This level of stress might not be great for everyone, but it should be. Why? Because your customers (both internal and external) are more important than your CEO or the CEO's family members. You must set the tone and be the example 100% of the time you're in front of your customers.

My coping mechanism to ensure I was always 'on' was to assume I was on camera at all times, that the CEO or my boss was watching my every move. This helped me manage my stress levels when people really were watching. It showed in the way I acted and delivered. You don't get to choose to be the example; you have to be!

THE EXAMPLE FOR YOUR FAMILY

Building your character can't happen without being the best version of yourself not only at work, but at home. Work-life balance is something a lot of us retail leaders struggle with— we get home from a long day, and we have nothing left to give.

Kids often act out in their safe space. So, if your child is tough to handle after school, it's likely because they've been keeping it together all day. When they get home, they feel safe, let their guard down, and that's when the chaos starts.

Adults aren't so different. If you follow the steps in this book, being intentional and conscious every minute of your workday, chances are, you'll be out of patience by the time you get home. You'll be in your safe space and might start acting unconsciously, not communicating with your loved ones with the same thoughtfulness and care you showed all day. Just like when your kid comes home from school, your own storm begins.

It's all about the mantra "work hard, play hard." Playing hard doesn't just mean finding fun activities; it also relates to the time you spend with family and friends. You're not off the clock when you get home. Just like you schedule breaks throughout your workday, you need to schedule breaks at home too. These scheduled breaks are your moments to truly relax. To achieve the so-called work-life balance, you have to be as intentional and conscious with your family time as you are at work.

I emphasize this because your peak productivity at work is linked to your happiness at home.

When it comes to work-life balance, it's a bit of a misnomer. I prefer to call it work-life integration. Sometimes work might require 60-70%, even 80% of your time, leaving less for home life. At other times, it could be the other way around, where you lean into your home life more. Typically, your first year in a new role will demand more from you at work, but as you progress, you'll find more time for your family. It's important to communicate this cycle with your family.

I'm fortunate to be married to a fellow retailer who gets this dynamic. If your partner isn't in the same field, explaining this to them is crucial. As each year progresses, you should be able to be more present at home. It's not that you're working less in years two, three, or four; it's that you're more aware and in control, allowing you to be clearer and bring less work home.

AN EXAMPLE WORTH FOLLOWING

Who exactly are you being the example for, at any given moment?

Simple: the person right in front of you at that time (even if it's yourself, looking in the mirror).

I've always gotten into trouble for not responding quickly to emails and not picking up my phone when bosses call. This happens because if a customer is in front of me, they get my undivided attention. If a team member is in front of me, they get my undivided attention too. The emails and phone calls can wait. What example am I setting if I immediately stop a conversation to answer my boss's call and then spend 30 minutes at the front of the store talking about something irrelevant to what they need from me at that moment? By not looking at my phone during my 2–3 hour visit or by not checking emails, I'm showing that the person with me at that moment is the most important. I am there for them.

For those who travel and lead teams they seldom see, this example is crucial. You need to set boundaries. Your bosses and business partners should know when you are "out of office" because you are present for those you are with. Everyone should know when you check and respond to emails. To increase your followers and develop many in your future, this approach is key. People come first, and those looking you in the face at the moment are the most important at that time.

I remember traveling with a new Human Resource partner of mine. We had a 6-hour training session with a full team of store managers in Boston, Mass. After the session, at dinner, he told me how impressed he was that I hadn't looked at my phone once. He mentioned he hadn't seen anyone at my level do that before and how hard it was for him to adopt the same approach due to what others demanded of him and what he thought he should demand of himself. I appreciated his feedback and example because his vulnerability made him one of my best business partners, and it also reminded me of the importance of this approach.

People learn more effectively by seeing rather than being told. They need to see your leadership coming from you, not from your words, directions, even commands.

When a leader acts in a way that's worth following, it

becomes clear to everyone else what is expected and valued. In being the example, you're unlocking each of their growth. You're allowing them to get unstuck and progress in their own journey.

And that's what you're after. A great leader makes more great leaders.

Lao Tzu, the author of the Tao Te Ching, puts it best:

A leader is best when people barely know he exists, when his work is done, his aim fulfilled, they will say: *we did it ourselves.*

CHAPTER FOUR

BE ACCOUNTABLE

Accountability is a prerequisite for success.

Without it, your results are completely out of your hands and in the hands of everyone else. I don't know about you, but I prefer to be in control of my own destiny. In order to have that control, I need to acknowledge that I, and only I, am responsible for everything I do.

I once coached a newly promoted DM whose entire life was centered around being a victim. Every moment of every day, she was finding reasons why things weren't happening, why she wasn't getting results, and why none of it was her fault.

She was going nowhere with that mindset. She was putting so much energy into not taking accountability, she had no energy left to solve problems when they came up.

Contrast that example with another manager I was coaching. I did a store visit one day, and the manager was two hours late. I was waiting outside the whole time, wondering: where the hell is this guy? Is he seriously just not coming? Finally he came walking up the sidewalk. He saw me and immediately his face hardened.

I didn't give him hell. I said, "Let's just get the store open." Focus on solving the problem first, then coach.

Once the store was open, I asked him, "What happened this morning?"

He told me, "Look, I have no excuse. I should have made it on time. It won't happen again."

"Okay," I said. "I'll trust you on that." We moved on with the work day.

It wasn't until I got home that night that I found out the truth. His car had broken down. He had been taking the bus two hours each way, every day, to get to work. And he was too proud to admit he was taking the bus—not to mention being worried that if I found out he didn't have a car, I'd demote him out of management.

But I wouldn't even think of doing that. In taking accountability for what happened and simply saying, "It won't happen again," his character shone through as exactly the kind of person I wanted heading up the store. A lot of other bosses might have written him off—he was two hours late, he's lazy, he doesn't have a car, he's out. But his character, shown by his accountability, was what mattered.

If you have good character, everything else is teachable. And accountability is what makes or breaks character.

VICTIM BEHAVIORS

Being a victim is like being out of gasoline. You aren't going anywhere.

When you are accountable you have the fuel necessary to get to your destination. How far you progress will depend on how accountable you are. Think octane for a vehicle; are you filling your car up with 87 or 94 octane? It will make a difference.

A huge obstacle to success is a lack of accountability for the things we did wrong early in our careers. We tend to think that because we were less skilled at one point, we deserve to be less successful now or later in our lives. But this is not true. Once you acknowledge and embrace your past or present situation, you'll find solutions and make things happen for yourself. So, stop letting your past or present situation beat you down and keep you from recognizing your potential and reaching your capacity. Start now!

Many years ago, I had an Area Manager in North Carolina who was directly managing one store while being responsible for two more. She was a talented store manager with the potential to do more. Back then, retailers didn't have recruiters. We did all the recruiting ourselves, and it was one of the toughest parts of being a District Manager at the time. You had to be good at it to succeed.

This Area Manager lost some talent and ended up with only

3 to 4 total managers across the three stores. She looked to me for help and support in recruiting talent. I gave her none. Instead, I guided her verbally, listened, and encouraged her based on her ideas for finding talent. She had to run her store and keep the other two afloat while finding about five management members to join the team. This was a hard moment for her, and honestly, for me too, because I knew this was the development she needed. Inside, I knew if I helped her, it would get done faster and be less painful for her. But she needed to learn how to overcome these obstacles with three stores if she was ever going to successfully lead 10 to 12.

She learned how to cold call (before LinkedIn existed) from the sales floor while coaching sales associates. She held interviews on the sales floor. Once she had no other option than to acknowledge and embrace her reality, she found solutions and made it happen, not only for her then but for many years to come as a successful District Manager and eventually a Recruiter.

Being a victim means allowing someone else to control the narrative of your life. Victim behaviors are all about things happening to you. Here are some common examples.

UNAWARE AND UNCONSCIOUS

It was the mid-nineties and I was driving my Regional Director and President of the company to a store visit in

Scottsdale, Arizona. From the backseat, the President was challenging me on my denim business.

I immediately defended my results by saying, "we are completely sold out of sizes". The conversation shifted to something else, and I figured I had deflected well enough.

That was until we got out of the car in the parking lot and my Regional Director pulled me aside to let me know how poor my response was and why. He told me that I, like most field leaders, tended to exaggerate in order to get my point across. He proceeded to share that in doing so, I lose credibility; I needed to be specific in my answers if I want to get others to believe me, not only in the conversation but in general.

I had succeeded my entire career for the most part up to this point based on my salesmanship, however I was completely unaware how my selling nature could be perceived to those not wanting to be sold to.

We will all be unaware and unconscious of things at times. Sure, it helps to have people around you that will be honest with you; however the best way for you to be aware and conscious without relying on others is to constantly be curious.

PERSONAL EXCUSES

I remember one day heading to work, stuck in traffic, I knew I was going to be late for work (maybe this is another reason why I didn't give the two-hours-late store manager a hard time when I was in the boss role). The entire time I was rehearsing in my head what I was going to say.

I arrived at work, made sure I ran in so they saw me sweat a bit, and immediately went into a rant about how bad traffic was and how I had left my house in plenty of time.

My boss's response: "You obviously didn't leave early enough."

People don't care about what kept you from delivering, they care that you know what kept you, that you own it, and that you do it differently the next time.

I never again blamed traffic for being late. I began to anticipate traffic even if it didn't exist, and ended up showing up to work early most shifts—and when traffic was worse than expected, I showed up just in time.

This mindset works for all other excuses. Think about the "my dog ate my homework" excuse. Well, maybe you shouldn't have left your homework where your dog could get it. What about the "The ref got the call wrong"; maybe you shouldn't have allowed the game to be that close to begin where one bad call could determine the outcome.

"I CAN'T"

Well then you won't. It's that simple. When you say you can't, your mind won't look to figure out how and your body will sit in atrophy.

I believed I could do anything until I was about 30 years old. This attitude and language propelled me to become a 21 year old district manager and 25 year old regional director. Once I hit 30 years of age, I remember starting to believe that my lack of a college education would get in the way of me progressing past this point. I remember saying to myself, "I can't communicate with the Harvard MBA graduates, and they will never give me additional responsibilities".

I essentially sat in atrophy for 10 years as a Regional Director until I finally broke through at the age of 35 to become the Director of North American stores for Urban Outfitters. This breakthrough happened 3 years prior when I changed my thinking and therefore changed my language.

Once I said that I could, I did. And so can you.

ACCOUNTABILITY BEHAVIORS

Your body's actions reflect the words you use. When you make excuses, your actions align. The opposite is also true. The key to mastering accountability starts with mastering your language.

With accountability behaviors, it's all about things happening because of you, not to you. Here's how to start.

ACKNOWLEDGE REALITY

This is where winning starts.

I like to refer to the glass as half, not half full or not half empty. You can only solve for what's real. I used to blame the weather, not how to win with the weather. I used to blame other people's emotions, not how to influence them.

The weather is what it is and the other person's emotions are what they are. You can't progress if you don't acknowledge these things. Once you do, and only then, can you move towards making shit happen for yourself.

Once I acknowledged my lack of a college degree for example, I could start to solve for my communication opportunities. It was what it was.

Acknowledging reality is when your mind gets involved in accepting what is. Embracing reality is when your heart gets involved in accepting it, too. It's when your emotions start to enter the picture, rather than just the rational mind accepting it. You'll need both your mind and heart all in to start to find solutions.

EMBRACE REALITY

I always knew I didn't have a college degree and this reality didn't bother me until it did. When it didn't bother me, it wasn't an obstacle and I progressed nicely. The minute I began wishing things were different, aka not embracing my reality, things slowed down and I couldn't seem to get out of my own way.

I like to think of acknowledging reality as seeing it. Embracing reality is when you can feel it. Acknowledging is the what and Embracing is the why.

I remember when I was a store manager with a strong desire to get promoted to district manager. I was the second best store manager in the region at the time—another manager named Hector was #1. It wasn't until I embraced this reality that I realized my next step.

FIND SOLUTIONS

Once I embraced where I stood in the lineup, I knew what I had to do. I had to learn from Hector so I could add what he offered into my toolbox—and I had to leverage what I had that he didn't. I was mobile to anywhere, and he was never going to leave the ability to surf on a daily basis.

We became good friends, supporting each other's careers. We knew we were not competing for the same job, and could help each other get where we both wanted. I began watching the way he led and marketing my mobility to anyone who would listen.

MAKE IT HAPPEN

Hector and I embraced our reality, became good friends

and ultimately both became district managers and more. We learned from each other and I moved out of state while he remained at home near the beach. We both made it happen for ourselves.

THE POWER OF YET

Your mind and heart take what you say and think seriously. They can't tell the difference, and your actions typically follow suit. When you say or think you're scared of something, your actions will align with that. When you say or think you're not good at communication, your actions will align with that too. Why would anyone want their mind or heart to think or feel as if they aren't good at something? Only when it's true because then you can act and develop on it, otherwise you're putting yourself at a massive disadvantage in life because your mind and heart control your actions.

I don't necessarily believe in manifesting, but I do believe you act on what you say and think. If you say and think positive things about yourself, you'll walk with more swagger than if you say or think the opposite. To progress in your current role or into others, having a positive self-image is extremely important. People want to work with winners and those they feel smart following.

Personal examples include, "She'll never like me," meaning

you won't find out because your heart can't take the possible rejection. "I'll never be able to do that" means you won't try because your heart can't handle the possible defeat. On the flip side, "She'll like me" means you will attempt to find out and "I can do that" means you will try. Sure, in both cases maybe she won't like you and you didn't do it, but what good ever comes from not finding out? Nothing.

In my career, when I felt my lack of a college education meant I wasn't intelligent enough to communicate with those who had degrees at the highest levels, I avoided having conversations. My actions were in alignment with my words and thoughts. The opposite was also true. At points in my career, I thought I wasn't a good salesman, operator, or merchant and in those instances, I wasn't because I avoided certain things.

As children, we think and say negative thoughts about ourselves all the time. Sometimes it's because we believe them and other times it's because we want attention (unconsciously) from our parents, teachers, or coaches. As adults, we tend to do it for the same reasons. Either we have grown to believe it by thinking or saying it for many years, or we want attention (unconsciously) from our spouses, bosses, or peers.

To take control of your own life and career, you must think positively about yourself to walk in the direction of where you want to be. The best way to get to where you want to be is to be walking in that direction.

I always find it fascinating how hard it is for people to say thank you when offered a compliment. People, myself included, tend to feel embarrassed and find a way not to acknowledge it. This is because we aren't used to saying positive things about ourselves out loud. What you think to yourself matters, but what you say out loud is even more important.

The most important underutilized word in the vocabulary is "yet." It should be added at the end of every sentence where you are thinking or saying out loud what you don't have or haven't done.

Examples are, "I don't have the car I want yet," "I am not where I want to be in my career yet," "My work-life balance isn't what I want yet," "I can't bench press 225 yet," "I can't seem to eat healthy yet," etc.

Since our minds and hearts take everything literally and don't know the difference, they will walk in the direction of the comments made. If you add "yet" to the end of each of these comments, your mind and heart will see a pathway and keep walking in the appropriate direction, one foot in front of the other.

Most people are never satisfied and therefore make comments that align with not being satisfied, and these comments can stifle your progress toward receiving or achieving the things you want. It's not about manifesting something to happen in your life; it's about ensuring that your language generates the correct footsteps.

My son is 10 at the time of me writing this book, and he currently has a fixed mindset. He thinks any failure is representative of who he is rather than a result of a particular action. I have found that helping him add "yet" to things is helping him feel as if he still can do or get what he currently doesn't have, and I see him walking in the correct direction.

Personally, when I thought I wasn't a good operator, I avoided all things operations. When I worked for Dave Temple, he made it very clear that I wasn't good at operations yet and would have to be to progress.

It's important as a leader to not only be conscious of the thoughts and words we use, but also the thoughts and words we allow those we are accountable for to use. It starts by not allowing anyone to say anything fixed and coaching our teams to use the word "yet."

AN ACCOUNTABLE LEADER

In order to make it happen for yourself and others, you have to first find yourself north of the accountability line, emotionally connected with your reality so you can see and feel more clearly what you have to do.

Accountability in leadership is like the glue that holds everything together in a team or an organization. It's about being responsible for what you do, the decisions you make, and how those decisions affect your team. When leaders are accountable, they set the stage for a culture of trust and reliability, important for any successful team.

I have found, like with most things, being accountable has its pivotal moment, the shifting point.

You may find solutions and make things happen without acknowledging or embracing your reality, but it will be a flash in the pan and not sustainable because you just happen to be in the right place at the right time (which at times is a skill in itself, but not for this context).

If you want to drastically improve your odds, you must acknowledge and embrace your reality. This is when you understand your current state of affairs and can determine an appropriate course of action.

I find shifting from simply acknowledging to embracing reality is a sticking point for most people and really holds folks back from delivering peak performances.

If you simply acknowledge the reality, you may think and say out loud how much you dislike the reality, and since your mind and heart take what you say and think literally, they won't be excited about walking in the direction they need to be walking in.

When you embrace it, make it your favorite, so to speak, you create the conditions for your mind and heart to get you moving in the right direction.

Someone might acknowledge that it's raining but not find a way to take advantage of it until they embrace it. Someone might acknowledge the real estate market is crashing rather than embrace it and find a solution to take advantage of it.

Acknowledging alone, to me, is half the battle. It's the mind's acceptance only. The heart's acceptance comes with embracing it. You need both to really ensure you are putting one foot in front of the other and walking in the right direction.

Before I was let go from my role as a Regional Director when I was 30 years old, I accepted that I struggled with merchandising women's fast fashion, but I didn't embrace it. Therefore, I mentally knew I needed to strengthen this skill set but lacked the emotional connection to it. Because I lacked the emotional connection (the embrace), I didn't move in the direction I needed to. I remained in purgatory.

I had a General Manager who was more than capable of being a District Manager. They were not mobile to opportunities and therefore were going to have to sit tight for quite some time. For some time, they accepted this reality, but their performance began to slip. Why? Because they didn't fully embrace this reality. I had to ensure they emotionally connected to the reality and understood how to leverage it to continue to grow themselves and others. They needed to be an active participant in the reality and not a bystander.

I had a district manager who had been a district manager for 7 years with another company before working with me. She was a General Manager who I promoted pretty quickly to a District Manager again. In the beginning, I let her know that I thought she was leading like a first-year DM and needed to think and speak differently. She had 7+ years of experience in the role and, regardless of how long she had been in this role with this company, she needed to walk and talk like a 7+ year district manager. She needed to think this about herself internally and speak this way externally. Once she started to do this, you could see her 7+ years of experience exude itself, and peers and other supervisors started to take notice. I didn't do anything other than redirect the language. She did the work. We need to either tell ourselves to knock it off and think and say the right things, or we have to ensure others in our hemisphere do.

Leaders who hold themselves accountable are great role models. They show their team how to be responsible and reliable. It's like setting a standard: "This is how we do things here." It helps everyone understand what's expected of them, and it pushes the whole team to be better.

If you're not ready to face your current situation head-on, figuring out any kind of solution is going to be tough. You might not even be tackling the right problem, let alone figuring out how to solve it. And when it comes to getting stuff done, remember, people aren't interested in excuses. They want to know what you're going to do next, or how you're going to change things up to make it happen. Plus, if climbing up the career ladder is on your mind, being accountable is non-negotiable. It's the deal-breaker that will keep you stuck or let you break out and run.

CHAPTER FIVE

BE DISCIPLINED

With the first four practices, you've strengthened your foundation. You've proven to yourself and others that you're capable of doing the hard work. You've shown an openness to learn, to fill your cup. You've set a best-in-class example and made sure you're doing the right work before pointing fingers at others.

Before you can become an upperclassman, so to speak, you need to create habits, disciplines, and get your mind, body, and soul in a place to handle all the inputs that will come your way once you graduate from this step.

Let's talk about habits, or what some may call routines. What you used to do in a less organized way early in your role or career won't cut it anymore, as more is expected of you and your influence over others becomes more apparent.

Take my example of a morning routine:

My morning routine has become the most important part of my entire day. I tell myself I need 6 to 7 hours of sleep. So, if I go to bed at 10 pm, I set the alarm for either 4 or 5 am, depending on what I want to accomplish the next morning. If I stay up until 11 pm, then it's 6 hours of sleep because I don't sleep past 5 am. I usually carry this into my weekends as well.

Why so early? Most professions require a warm-up. Think about sports or acting—they don't just start cold; they spend time priming themselves for the game, theater, or camera.

Retail or leadership shouldn't be any different. It's a game too, and if you're asked to both coach and play, as many of you are, priming yourself is even more important. You need to be ready not just for your own productivity but for the productivity of others as well.

I start with an hour all to myself, before my wife or son wakes up when I'm at home. I take care of the dogs, then sit and enjoy a nice cup of coffee, preferably outside if the weather allows. When I can, I fit in 20 minutes of meditation during this hour. Then, I hit the gym or go for a run for an hour to 90 minutes. After that, it's back to the house or hotel room for a shower, and then I'm off to win the day.

I'm up and moving for 3 hours before I enter the "stadium" that is my workplace. I count commute time as work, whether it's on a train, plane, or in an automobile. I use this time to either work on myself with inputs from an audiobook and podcasts or outputs like emails or calls to people I work with. I am working from the time I walk out of the hotel lobby or front door until I land back at my destination or re-enter my house at the end of the day.

Now, about the discipline associated with habits. We've all heard it takes 30, 45, or 15 days to create a habit—there are many blogs and books on the subject. I don't know the exact time it takes to form a habit, but I do know if you're not disciplined in doing what needs to be done, even when you don't want to, the time it takes doesn't matter.

Health is crucial at this stage of your journey. What you influence others to do becomes more important than what you're capable of doing yourself. You've built your character to earn the right to lead and influence. You might wonder, especially if you've been in leadership roles for years, why you need to do all this freshman and sophomore work, even in a new role with the same responsibilities at a different company. It's about proving your character to yourself for confidence, and to others for their confidence in you.

To lead and influence effectively, you need to be in good physical, mental, and spiritual health. This doesn't mean you have to be a bodybuilder or a monk. It means getting your blood flowing, clearing your mind, and believing in something bigger than what you know (belief).

I recall this transition in my career. Like many, I used to stay up until 2, 3, maybe even 5 in the morning and still be productive the next day. But I realized, sure I was productive, but

I could've been better. When it was just me on commission sales, making money off my salesmanship, it was fine. But once I realized I wasn't creating the best environment for those I led to be successful because I wasn't the best version of myself, I knew I had to change my health habits.

Discipline also involves learning to cope in healthy ways. We're familiar with plenty of unhealthy coping mechanisms, but to be disciplined, find the healthy alternatives. (My undiagnosed ADHD was actually an advantage in this way; I had to figure out for myself how to cope and stay on target.)

Here are the main steps you need to focus on to build this practice.

TIME MANAGEMENT

When I was 21 and in my first district manager role, I quickly learned that my time management skills needed work. I went from managing one store to overseeing 12 stores in Arizona and New Mexico. Back then, we didn't have Area Managers or District Managers in Training, so the jump between these two roles was the biggest of any in my career. Around the same time, I came across a concept called "the bowling ball rule".

The rule basically said that you can only put so many bowling balls in a box, but you can fit an enormous amount of marbles in that same box. The bowling balls represented the tasks or deadline-driven projects that needed to be accomplished, while the marbles were the in-between work that didn't necessarily have a deadline but still needed to be done.

This tool or theory not only helped me with time management but also turned out to be one of the biggest game changers for those I led. I was able to teach my store leaders how to spend their time more effectively and accomplish much more in a day.

You might fit maybe 1, 2, or 3 bowling balls or deadline tasks into a day (high ROI work), but you could fit 10, 20, or even 30 marbles or in-between tasks into the same day. The idea was to list out the in-between work in order of importance. We either allocated 3 to 5 tasks per associate for each downtime period or made the list visible to all and turned it into a fun competition to see who could complete more tasks throughout the day.

Outworking, Outlearning, Being Accountable, and Being the Example are easy when you have all the time in the world. When you are single without any kids or other responsibilities you can work 60+ hours a week. You have time on your side.

When you layer in a partner, child or any other high priority you will be required to outwork, outlearn, be accountable, and be the example in what at times will feel like very narrow limits.

I highly recommend that if you don't have other priorities that you learn how to manage your time more wisely so you can use your free time more effectively and also just be that much more productive.

This is where you really learn productivity: you don't have the option to not be there for your family, and you don't have the option to not be there for your work. It's a forcing function, and learning time management is like fuel for discipline.

A big piece of this is killing your perfectionism. Don't let perfect be the enemy of good. Take a shorter amount of time to deliver 75% of the work at an excellent A level, not a longer amount of time to deliver all the work, but at a C level.

HEALTH

Discipline really comes down to the right habits and routines, plus staying active. In my experience, both mental and physical fitness are crucial—and by fitness, I mean just moving around or eating right most of the time. And yeah, I enjoy a good piece of fried chicken too. Staying fit and healthy increases your capacity and patience, making you a better leader. Let me give you an example.

Back when I started in retail, I used to work out after work. It gave me the energy to party all night. But as I got older and more mature, I shifted my workouts to the morning. I realized I needed that energy for my workday, not for my evenings.

Whether it's eating right or working out, being active clears my mind. I can listen better, think more clearly, and react more effectively. I've seen leaders who aren't very healthy—not necessarily unfit, but maybe they're always snacking on chips, sitting all day without moving much. This often leads to exhaustion and even short-temperedness. But for me, physical activity has always been important. It makes you more agile and better able to handle situations.

Later in my career, I realized the importance of mindfulness. I started to meditate—not that everyone needs to—but being able to observe and understand your own thoughts is crucial, especially in retail leadership. When you're responsible for others, recognizing your inner voice and ensuring you're thinking the right things before you speak is key. Being mindful helps you be aware of your thoughts, allowing you to articulate what's necessary, rather than just speaking your mind impulsively.

LIFESTYLE

The retail career lifestyle often looks and feels quite different from a corporate one (although I've never been in the corporate life—this is just what I hear). There are more late nights, more travel...and more socializing. More partying, especially earlier in people's careers at the store level and district level. This lifestyle requires you to be really disciplined during your working hours.

As I moved up in my career, I realized that my ultimate responsibility was to those I led. I needed to be in the right frame of mind and physically prepared every morning to be the best version of myself. This meant eating the right foods, ensuring some kind of movement, and being mindful of my actions. When I was 21, I started exploring Eastern philosophy, learning about Yin and Yang, and understanding that what goes up must come down. This helped me not get too worked up about wins or losses.

I learned that to be your best self for the team you lead, you can't party until the early hours and then show up at work at 6 AM. At some point, you recognize that if you want to advance in your career, you need to be more clear-headed in the mornings. Movement is one of the most important things for every human to do; for years I used to wake up 30 minutes before I had to leave the house, just enough time to take a quick shower, brush my teeth and go. One day I decided I was going to wake up early enough to workout, something I used to do after the workday was done. I started waking up with enough time to enjoy a cup of coffee in the morning, make it to the gym, shower and then go to work.

Being mindful and getting daily movement improve your odds of success and create better conditions for winning. Specifically, in retail leadership, being positive is essential to lift others up. Retail is an environment where improvisation and thinking on your feet are crucial, and it's so focused on being with people.

I remember a time when I showed up for work grumpy, and my district manager pointed out that I must not have worked out that morning. At that point, I had built a character for myself that was disciplined in working out. It was a good reminder of how important physical activity is for my mindset. Typically, I find that people who get movement in the morning are in the best frame of mind. It was also a good reminder that when people trust the character you've built, you'll find yourself surrounded by advisors helping to propel you forward.

Early on, learning about Eastern philosophy, particularly Taoism, was a game-changer for me. It helped me remain calm and not get too high or too low. This mindfulness, along with physical activity, has been vital. It's given me the stamina to be my best self throughout the day and known for being high energy right until the end.

DISCIPLINED ROUTINES

Discipline doesn't come naturally to any of us. Don't worry, you're not alone in that.

But discipline is a key ingredient of your Retail Leader Roadmap. So you need to figure out the routines that will enable you to stay disciplined. Routines are like a shield. Think of them as your personal set of guidelines, a way to navigate through the chaos of daily life without letting your feelings hijack your productivity and focus. They offer a stable, consistent path when everything else might be in flux, ensuring that you stay on track even on your toughest days.

Remember, time is a more precious commodity than money. While money can fluctuate, time, once spent, is gone forever. That's why it's crucial to invest your time wisely, and routines are the perfect tool for this. They help you allocate your time effectively, ensuring that every minute counts. With a well-structured routine, you can make the most out of each day, turning time into an ally, not an enemy.

Above all, routines are instrumental in maintaining your health—the bedrock on which your ability to lead sits. A healthy lifestyle fueled by consistent routines boosts your energy levels, sharpens your focus, and enhances your decision-making abilities. It's not just about the physical aspect; mental and emotional health also thrives on the stability that routines provide.

In essence, by nurturing your health through routines, you're laying the foundation for strong, effective leadership.

PILLAR ONE WRAP-UP

Your retail leadership career is a zero sum game. There's a competition factor; if you don't get an opportunity, it means someone else did. Competing is all about hard work, always evolving, bringing your best self, being accountable, and staying disciplined. Think about it: have you ever won anything, in any competition, without showing these qualities? I'm not just talking about stepping up to get a bronze medal. I'm talking about aiming for at least silver, but really gunning for the gold.

So, ask yourself these five questions:

1. Can I work harder?

2. Can I learn more?

3. Can I set a better example?

4. Can I be more accountable?

5. Can I be more disciplined?

THE RETAIL LEADER'S ROADMAP

If you answer 'yes' to any of these, then you know you've got more to give to up your game.

Then, think about this: Is there anyone in your line of work who works harder than you, learns more than you, sets a better example than you? If the answer is 'yes', then you've got a real-life example to look up to. You can learn from them and figure out how to step up your own performance. Remember, there's always room for improvement, and someone else's success can be a great motivator for your own journey.

BUILD YOUR CONNECTIONS

THE SOFT SKILLS ARE WHERE YOU START TO INCORPORATE OTHER PEOPLE INTO YOUR SUCCESS EQUATION. THESE ARE YOUR INTERPERSONAL SKILLS. THE TRAITS AND ATTRIBUTES YOU USE TO INTERACT AND COMMUNICATE WITH PEOPLE. YOU CAN GROW TO A POINT RELYING ON HARD SKILLS; HOWEVER, YOU WON'T BE SUCCESSFUL LEADING OTHERS WITHOUT THE SOFT SKILLS. YOU WILL BE STUCK CONTRIBUTING TO SOMEONE ELSE'S LEADERSHIP.

IF YOU'RE NOT ALIGNED WITH YOUR BOSS, AND THEY'RE NOT ALIGNED WITH YOU, YOU'RE STUCK.

CHAPTER SIX

DEVELOPMENT

In order for the soft skills to translate to others, you must have already developed your solid character. For soft skills to land, people have to respect you and see that they can get something from you. This is why when you start a new job, get a new boss or lead a new team, you have to re-exhibit the hard skills to earn the respect of the new folks now in your hemisphere. Re-exhibiting is easy, if you have truly developed the hard skills, because they are always present in the way you do what you do.

When you have shown people that you consistently work hard, are open to learning, set an example, are accountable and self-disciplined, they will listen to what you have to say. They will also forgive you as you make mistakes developing these skills.

Once you've mastered the above, it's time to Build Your Connections.

Building your Connections is made up of three key practices:

1. Development

2. Communication

3. Influence

First, you will have to acknowledge your privilege as a leader, then understand the many hats you must wear to effectively lead your team.

No longer are you the most important person in the room, you are now accountable to the most important people in the room. This means that your ability to grow the capability of others becomes your primary function. Up until now, you were able to focus primarily on delivering results by your own hands and now all of your results will come from the hands of others.

Communication will need to become your biggest strength. This is where you will need to begin to really roll your sleeves up. This is where you will flex your hard skills again. You will have to work harder than anyone at this, be more open to learning regarding it than anyone else. You will need to set an example as a great communicator at all times and hold yourself accountable for every word that comes out of your mouth.

Most people assess their communication skills based on what they say and not how people respond. This is where most people fail at communication. I like to refer to it as, "getting it off their chest". Just because you said it, may mean you communicated it, but it doesn't mean you successfully communicated it. Communication is as much about what you observe in other people's body language and responses as it is what comes out of your mouth.

If you want to be great at leading people in any profession, you need to be successful with communication. This is where learning how to respect your own personality, selfishness, ego and emotions come into play. Once you understand and respect your own tendencies, you can then, and only then, understand and respect other people's tendencies. This is where the magic happens and this is what separates good from great leaders.

FIRST: ACKNOWLEDGE YOUR PRIVILEGE

Working in retail is a privilege, and if you're leading others, you're even more privileged.

In my over 30 years in retail, I've always been amazed hearing stories about people not showing up, cutting out early, or ending up at a bar at 2pm when they're supposed to be in a store, cubicle, or corner office. Or shopping for hours instead of spending time in their own stores with their teams.

Leading someone is a privilege that shouldn't be taken lightly.

Once, my Human Resource team conducted an exercise with us. We all stood in a row, arms locked, from left to right. For each question asked, if your answer was 'YES', you stepped forward. If 'NO', you stepped back. Questions included things like, "Did either of your parents attend college?" or "Have you ever feared for your life when pulled over by a police officer?" After about 15 to 20 questions, it was clear who had grown up the most privileged and who the least privileged.

For a long time, I didn't like the word 'privilege'. I worked hard to get where I am and felt that being called privileged implied I hadn't earned it. But now, I understand what privilege really means and no longer dislike the term. It's just a word, after all.

I'm a white male who grew up in Stamford, Connecticut. This alone means I grew up privileged. I never had to worry about walking down the street in a hoodie, or fear being mistreated by police, earn less because of my gender, or be ridiculed for my sexuality.

I mention all this because as retail leaders, we're in a position to create privilege for others. Everyone we're responsible for should be able to say 'YES' to questions like, "Has a boss ever told you what you're good at and where you can improve?" or "Have you ever felt part of a team at work?" or "Have you worked somewhere that provided a safe space to relax off the clock?"

THE THREE HATS (PLAYER, COACH, GENERAL MANAGER)

Leading in retail is exceptionally hard because you are required to wear 3 different hats. You have to:

1. Play the Game

2. Coach the Team

3. Be the General Manager

Quick note: don't get confused here, all you retail leaders! I don't mean General Manager in the retail context. I mean General Manager in the sports context. In sports, the General Manager is the person responsible for player personnel.

If you're a store manager in a district with 10 stores, you're one of the 10 players on your district manager's team. You coach the team you lead, and you're also responsible for player personnel. This holds true whether you're a District Manager, Regional Director, or Vice President. You play on your boss's team and lead your own, while being accountable for your personnel.

Why is it tough to wear all these hats? Succeeding in each role requires different skills, and to excel in all three simultaneously, you need to know which role you're playing at any given time.

Since winning as a player hinges on having the right people, let's start with the role of being the general manager of your team.

GENERAL MANAGER

You'll make plenty of mistakes in your career, but getting it right when placing people in roles is vital. This is when you need to put on your general manager hat. And this is where you'll be spending the most time of the three hats, because it's about player personnel. This is a tough hat to wear; a lot of people prefer to just wear the Player and Coach hats. They're more fun. They don't require as many tough decisions and conversations. But if you're not wearing the General Manager hat, you're only doing two-thirds of the job, and you're not doing the most important third at all. You're ultimately stuck where you are, and you won't ascend as a leader.

HIRING

As a leader, placing people in positions is the most important decision you can make. You can't afford to deliver anything less than an A performance, which means you must get it right 9 out of 10 times, consistently.

Sure, you likely don't start out this way, but over time, if you have learned from your decisions, this type of performance is not only possible but required.

To reach the point where you are delivering an A performance, you need to review each hire and promotion retrospectively. Consider what questions you asked, how those who are succeeding answered them versus those who are not. Reflect on what observations you made, and what you saw in those succeeding versus those who are not.

You also have to trust your gut. Your gut is often correct, but not 9 out of 10 times consistently. A few of your gut calls will be wrong if you don't dig deeper, and since you're playing with your company's money, you can't afford to get this wrong more than 1 out of 10 times.

If you want the best odds of success when hiring from the outside, find a way to make it feel like it's from the inside. Get to know them in their environment if possible. If you can't, then getting references from people you already know and trust is the next best option. And if you can't get to know them in their environment and you don't have any personal references, then you have to rely on the interview or interviews.

The reason 80% of my questions are character-based is that connections and plans can be taught, while a person's character, which is the foundation, needs to already be in place.

You should ask the same initial questions of every candidate, though these may change based on the role. This gives you a baseline to work with when determining who to hire. Of course, based on the candidates' answers, you'll want to ask follow-up questions specific to each candidate, so these will change from one candidate to another.

The most important thing I've learned over the years is how to ask the right questions, and funnily enough, I learned this when I was the one being interviewed.

When I lost my job at 30, I hadn't interviewed for a position in 13 years. The last time I interviewed for a job was as an Assistant Store Manager, and here I was, a Regional Director with 5 years of experience. I had been promoted to each role I ever had. I earned my roles and didn't talk anyone into believing in me. I thought, now what? Shit. I hate selling myself.

I struggled mightily in my interviews. I had been successful interviewing others, so why was I struggling to be interviewed? It was because I was inexperienced on this side of the table, and also I had been able to show my worth in the past, not just sell it.

The reality is the interviewee has to sell themselves. I read about how George Clooney changed his approach to auditioning from trying to impress the casting agents to becoming the solution the casting agents were looking for. He realized that they needed to find the right actor as much or more than he needed to get the role. This approach helped me come to terms with selling myself.

I also quickly realized that when I was asked hypothetical questions, which was 90+% of the time, I struggled answering them. I found myself reaching for answers, reaching for what the interviewer wanted to hear.

I decided I was no longer going to answer hypothetical questions and would only answer real-life scenario questions. This way, I would speak from experience, and the emotion and skills associated with each answer would be genuine and shine through.

For example, if I was asked how I would handle something in the new role, I would say something like, "I don't know exactly how I would handle it in this new role, but let me tell you how I handled the same situation in my last role." In doing this, I was able to paint a picture for the interviewer, almost as if they were observing it.

Quickly after landing my new role with Urban Outfitters, I began approaching interviews this way. I would only ask questions about the person's past to paint a picture for myself. I would ask how they handled their first 90 days in their last role, not how they would handle the first 90 in this new role. I would ask how they handled a performance problem in their recent role, not how they might in their new role. I would ask for specifics, preferably timeframes, names, etc. This way, they had to answer with real-life examples.

I also found that because I was so uncomfortable selling myself, many others might be as well, which is why I worked to make candidates as comfortable as possible. I have had peers and previous bosses tell me how they intimidate candidates a bit to see how much grit and determination they have. I don't find this to be helpful.

When candidates are comfortable and able to tell their real stories, it's the next best thing to actually having been able to observe them. This gives you the visual you need to make the most educated decision possible.

The biggest priority is assessing a person's character. Remember the foundational steps in this book. Do they work hard, learn, set the right example, hold themselves accountable, and exercise discipline? If they embody these five things, they have the character you want and the foundation to deliver anything.

PROMOTING

The biggest challenges I see leaders have when promoting internal talent are the following:

1. They skip the character review. They justify a person exhibiting less than all 5 characteristics because they

deliver certain results at the time. Maybe they work hard, but they are resistant to learning new things. Maybe they set a great example most of the time, but become a victim when pressured to improve something. People are most likely ready for next, when they are exhibiting the 5 characteristics and less likely when they are not. You are charged with people's livelihood and should play the better odds.

2. They assess the person's results based on their results versus the results of his or her team. Results come in many different forms and the results I am talking about here are the results of their skill development, not the metrics. Can he or she speak about the business exceptionally well while his or her team can't speak to their business at the same level? Does he or she work extremely hard however his or her team lacks the same work ethic? You should promote people because of what they can get others to do, not on what they can do themselves.

3. They don't ask his or her peers what they think. You should only promote people if they have a positive impact on those around them. I liken it to a Captains of sports team. They typically earn the C on the

Jersey because of the impacts he or she has on their teammates. Of course they deliver results as well, but it's the influence they have that earns them the promotion.

ASSESSING TALENT

No matter the team you have, you will always have someone force ranked at the top and the bottom. This assessment is critical because it gives you a baseline of current capabilities. The only way to truly progress is to constantly be upgrading your capabilities. Sure you might deliver improved results at times without expanding your capabilities on the team, but you won't be able to sustain the growth.

In the mid-nineties, Jack Welch was a vision of what a CEO should be in most people's eyes. In hindsight, maybe that shouldn't have been the case but nonetheless, I took a ton away from his teachings. Like most things, I didn't take his teachings literally—I ideated on them and made them work for me.

Jack Welch would force rank his team and bucket them into the top 20%, middle 70% and bottom 10%. He would require that each team replace the bottom 10% at the end of year with talent perceived to be an upgrade. He referred to 4 competencies that he deemed most important at the time when assessing versus solely looking at results. He talked a lot about how you should prioritize your time with the 3 different buckets of employees and the role each played on the team.

To me it wasn't about replacing the bottom 10% of your staff every year at review time in order to replace folks that were perceived to be more capable. I would force rank my team quarterly and look to coach folks up in order to have a different bottom 10% performer each quarter (and if there were folks who couldn't be coached up, of course it was my responsibility to further document things and often terminate their employment). The goal was to end the year with a bottom 10% performer who had a place on the team—preferably a bottom 10% performer who was stronger than anyone else's middle 70%.

When you coach a team, you want your worst performers to be better than the middle to top performers on other teams. For example, every baseball team's lineup has a player hitting 9th. A great baseball team will make sure that 9th hitter is better than the 4th or even 1st hitter on other teams.

Jack referenced a person's energy, ability to energize, the edge to make tough decisions and the ability to deliver on promises. I force ranked my team based on the practices mentioned earlier in this book. How hard they work, how open they are to learning, if they set the best example and hold themselves accountable, how disciplined they are. I found that if I could recognize which of these was the opportunity in someone and coach them up in this particular arena, the metrics would increase at the same time.

Each quarter I would force rank my team. If I had 10 direct reports for example, I would force rank them #1 thru #10. I would draw a line under my #2 representing my Top 20% and a line above my #10 represents the break between my middle 70% and bottom 10%.

My force rank is simple: I treat it like a draft.

Of the 10 direct reports, who would I protect and therefore they wouldn't be available to be chosen by another team. After I protected my first person, I would then ask myself who would I protect out of the 9 remaining direct reports until I got down to the last person at the end.

I primarily used the Character traits filter when determining who to protect. Who worked the hardest, was the most open to learning, set the best example, held themselves accountable the most, and was the most disciplined to the person who I thought did these things the least.

RETENTION MATTERS: HOW TO GROW PEOPLE WITHOUT DRIVING THEM AWAY

Anyone who's been a leader for any amount of time knows that it's easier to level folks up than it is to replace them. Sure, in some instances an external hire comes in and hits it out of the park and adds tremendous value to the team. (I would like to think that I was a valuable addition the few times I entered a new organization!)

But talent retention should be your main goal as a leader. When you retain talent and grow the majority of your talent internally, they will grow together. You can see what people are capable of, so that hiring becomes about selecting the best known quantity, rather than choosing the best of a set of strangers you haven't been able to observe.

Here's what to watch out for, though: the majority of people will come up short.

I've found that people typically fill up the time given with the work given. This means if you ask someone to do three things in a day, it will take them all day to do those three things. If I give you six things to do in a day, it will take you all day to do those six things.

Something similar happens when it comes to meeting expectations. In the previous example, people use all the time given to complete tasks. In this example, it's more about people feeling good enough about getting close.

You can reduce the expectation to ensure people can meet them, but I've found that if I reduce the expectations, they will still fall short of the new expectation by getting close again.

This is why finding the appropriate level of eustress—healthy psychological stress, or stretching your comfort zone—when developing people is important. How far can you positively push someone, and how far is too far?

You can only be successful in doing this if you pay close attention to your people's behaviors. This requires you to be present and focused on them, not just on yourself.

How can you tell when someone is being pushed too hard? They act out of character. If someone is usually chatty, they may become quiet and appear introverted. Someone who is usually calm and collected might become a bit irritable. This is when you stop and ask questions to understand where the unhealthy stress is coming from. Together, you might find solutions and keep pushing forward, or it might become clear that too much is being asked and the expectation needs to be pulled back a bit.

Why is it important to acknowledge and embrace that most people will get close, yet still miss expectations?

Because if you only reduce expectations, you'll just get less. If you can create the right eustress, you'll stretch people to not only deliver more but also grow more.

Also, you will still be able to recognize results that come up a little short because you'll find that they still make it to the podium.

BIASES

The current hot topic in Human Resources is biases. Companies are spending a lot of money on presentations and development to educate people on why it's important to not have biases.

But, like faking it 'till you make it, I call bullshit on this idea, too. We all have biases. I do, you do, and everyone in your work environment does. Companies want you to think biases are bad. The problem is, your biases have become part of your DNA.

Now, I don't condone all biases, but I believe they exist in everyone. I acknowledge and embrace this reality. When a company or someone doesn't acknowledge or embrace this fact, they can't find solutions. People get defensive when you insult their DNA, and that's when ego steps in. So if you don't want a defensive person in front of you, don't insult their DNA. Acknowledge it and discuss how they can best maneuver knowing this is a bias they have.

If you have a bias towards action, a person who seems less action-oriented might not progress on your team. But in fact, this person might be key to your team's success because they slow you and others down to ensure all angles are thought of before acting.

If you have a bias towards accommodation, someone who prefers to debate might not progress on your team. But in fact, this person might be key to your team's success because they ensure you're looking at all possible angles before acting.

It's not about whether a particular bias is good or bad. It's about the fact that biases exist, and when we tell people they shouldn't have them, they get defensive, and the possibility of working past it declines. When we acknowledge that biases exist, we can work within this reality to make great decisions and end up with a well-rounded team.

I have always had someone on my team who slows me down. They're often the operator, the debater, the more logical than emotional person. This person has been key on every team I've ever had. Without them, my ideas would bring as much trouble as they bring success.

DECISIONS

I was already a Regional Director for a few years when I came across the book Fierce Conversations by Susan Scott. The book had a lot of great nuggets, and the one that stood out to me the most was the chapter on the decision tree.

The decision tree is a reference tool to help determine the best way to make decisions. It was very handy at the time because I was starting to feel like I had more decisions to make that were more important to the organization's success. I needed to make sure I was using the company's money appropriately and teach those who worked for me to do the same.

Susan articulated this delegation model beautifully, in my opinion, and it's something I both use and teach to this day. In her words:

Picture your company as a tree. Each decision made affects the trees health to various degrees.

Leaf decisions are small decisions that won't have a major effect on the company. Yanking a leaf off a tree causes little to no harm. With increasing responsibility come branch decisions. Choices made at this level will certainly influence part of the company. Trunk decisions have a major effect on the company. Anything that touches the root of the tree has the potential to do major damage. The company's livelihood depends on decisions made at this level.

She then breaks down the decision tree into four parts:

1. The Leaf Decisions: Make the decision. Act on it. Don't report the action you took.

2. The Branch Decisions: Make the decision. Act on it. Report the action you took daily, weekly, monthly, or as appropriate.

3. The Trunk Decisions: Make the decision. Report your decision before you take action.

4. The Root Decisions: Make the decision jointly, with input from many people. These are the decisions that, if poorly made and implemented, could cause major harm to the organization.

I personally love how three of the four decision types require YOU to make the decision. It should be this way because you are in your position for a reason, and that's to make decisions and act. This is a skill you must excel at.

I learned when I needed to slow down and address Trunk or Root decisions differently than I had in the past. This is where taking a partner can really help ensure the decision is the best for the team and organization.

My father used to say, "Never let anyone put a monkey on your back." It meant, never let anyone who is supposed to make a decision have you make it for them. This decision tree really helped me hold people accountable for making decisions.

When people would come to me with Leaf decisions that needed to be made and would say something like, "I am not sure what to do here" or "What do you think I should do?" I would quickly say, "Sure you do," or "Don't ask me, this is a decision for you to make."

When people would come to me with a Branch decision that needed to be made and ask the same questions, I would simply tell them to make the decision they felt best about and let me know how it turned out afterward.

When people would come to me with a Trunk decision that needed to be made and ask the same questions, I would ask them what decision they thought was best and not fill in the blanks for them at any point. I might ask questions that help ensure they are thinking about everything when deciding what to do.

I learned over the years that different leaders put different decisions in different categories. One leader might believe a particular decision belongs in the Root category while another believes the same decision belongs in the Branch category.

One might argue that a decision a General Manager in a 1000-store chain makes is like a leaf decision to the company because it's 1/1000th. On the flip side, a decision a Senior Vice President makes might be a root decision based on its impact on the company. This is why decision quality is so important in a person's career. You can only progress as you build a track record of solid to great decisions.

Typically, CEOs and Chief Officers are tasked with these kinds of root decisions often. I find that when they push their agenda and just bring people along for the journey, they can get their company in some hot water. When they are presented with an idea or have an idea, the best in these roles spend time collaborating on the decision before moving forward.

COACH

Now that you have hired and promoted the right people. And now that you have an accurate assessment of what each person on your team can stand to improve in, it's time to coach them up.

The first and most important thing to do when coaching in retail is to flip the pyramid. You are at the bottom and those closest to the customer are at the top. You are in service to them and depending on what role you play, you pay different people to take care of them. For example, if you are a district manager with 10 stores. You pay 10 store managers a salary to provide the best experience for your customers which are both their support team and also the customers themselves.

This is why you should assess the caliber of your direct reports based on the performance of those they lead, not their individual performance. You should be constantly curious about what your direct reports can do more of or be better at. This way you can either reinforce behavior that will only continue to strengthen the internal and external customer experience or correct the behaviors getting in the way of a good experience for them.

- Flipping the pyramid does not mean you work for your direct report, it means you work for those you pay your direct report to take care of.

- Flipping the pyramid does mean that you understand that you are nothing without your direct reports and that you better pay real close attention to what they need to grow if you want to grow yourself and your customer satisfaction.

Now that we have the appropriate mindset about coaching. Let's talk about how to leverage the 20/70/10 model I mentioned earlier.

By design, your top 20% should help you develop your bottom 10% while inspiring and influencing your middle 70% to be better every day through his or her behaviors, actions and results. If you have a bottom 10% performer who you realize shouldn't be on your team or is on a performance management plan of some sort, don't leverage your Top 20% performers. Do it yourself.

You should spend the majority of your time with your top 20% performers. Most leaders get stuck spending most of their time with the problem performers and this stunts the growth of your best people, who in turn don't end up inspiring the majority of your team.

How can you spend the majority of your time with 2 to 4 people? Go to them, bring them to you, put them on projects that create the conditions for you to work with them remotely, and converse with them about the progress of the bottom 10%. Coach them how to influence your middle 70% through the way they work and how to develop peers who need what they have to offer.

PLAYER

Being presented with the opportunity to lead is a privilege.

And it should be taken seriously. If you aren't willing to focus on being a better version of yourself every day, you will let down others and minimize their capacity under your tutelage.

As a player on your boss's team, you have to deliver in your assigned role. For example, if you run a district, your district must perform well so your peers and your boss's team can succeed.

As the coach of your own team, you need to observe, assess, teach, and inspire results in those you lead. This is crucial for achieving the numbers required of you as a player. In retail, you're usually the only coach of your team. Unlike baseball, where there are hitting and pitching coaches, in retail, you often don't have a merchandising or operational coach to help improve specific skill sets. You have to level up your team yourself.

As the general manager of your team, you have to be objective and ensure you have the right players. It's rare for the coach and general manager to be the same person in sports, and when they are, it often doesn't work well. Coaches can develop biases and miss opportunities in people. A general manager is always scouting upcoming talent and working to upgrade every position for the present and future.

There's a fourth role that every player should aspire to: team captain. Over the years, I've had my teams watch the movie Miracle for talent inspiration. There are many incredible moments in that movie (give it a watch after Ted Lasso), but the captain of the team, Mike "Rizzo" Eruzione, has the storyline that I feel every team player can look to.

In the movie, Mike is close to being cut from the team by Coach Herb Brooks. It isn't until the final games before the Olympics that the coach decides to keep him on the team.

Mike struggles to score—Coach Herb refers to it as "Mike can't find the net"—in the games leading up to the Olympics, but he's also the glue that keeps the team moving forward. The team looks to him, and he pays as much attention to what others need as to what he needs.

The coach eventually decides to put Mike on the roster because of how he sees the rest of the team respond to him. And what happens? Mike ends up scoring the winning goal against the Soviet team to win the Gold Medal.

Your goal should be to be the captain of the team you're on, and also to both teach and expect everyone on your team to do the same.

It all starts with delivering results as a player. In leadership, you score points only when your team scores points. You'll only have people capable of scoring if you're objective and always looking to upgrade. Upgrading doesn't always mean replacing; it often means identifying an opportunity in someone and ensuring they get the necessary training.

AN OPEN BOOK TEST

The bottom line when it comes to developing people is that everything should be an open book test. There's no reason to keep the answers from anybody. Companies and leaders should be direct and clear about what's expected. It should be clear what an A, C, or F performance looks like.

You'll notice I didn't include a B or D grade. Why? Because I feel people give out these grades typically because they either grade too hard and don't want to give out A's, or they grade too softly and don't want to give out F's. To me, it's always been about doing it exceptionally well (A), getting it done (C), and missing the mark (F). I know a C doesn't feel great, but it's an average score, and just getting it done is average.

Growing up, my father didn't care about my grades as long as I came home with C's or better. He knew I didn't like school, and thanks to my ADHD personality, I would become bored easily if the teachers were not able to keep my attention. I typically received As in English and History because I enjoyed the information and tended to have really good teachers in these subjects. I typically struggled in math (outside of business math) and sciences.

Recently, I passed my real estate sales associate exam (always looking to expand the wellwisher company) and was reminded of how much I prefer to learn a certain way. I tried over and over again to read the textbook and then pass the quizzes at the end of each chapter only to fail over and over again. I couldn't retain the information.

Then, I decided to approach it the way I had done things in my past. I started at the end and worked backward. I studied the questions and answers. I would get 10 understood, then move on to the next 10, only to recap the full 20 before moving on to the next 10.

I got to the point, just by studying the answers, where I could get 1000 in a row correct while maybe only missing less than 10 total questions.

We need to make learning and retaining easy for folks in retail so they can spend their energy where it belongs: solving problems we don't know the answers to yet and getting the actual work done associated with the answers we are aware of.

The open book test concept is something that I love about retail. You can learn on the job. If you know what the answers are, you can spend your energy delivering them. If you don't know what the answers are, you might find yourself completely out of energy by the time you figure that out.

CHAPTER SEVEN

COMMUNICATION

I grew up being taught that your word was everything.

If you said it, you did it. No questions asked. Communication can make or break your credibility.

Not only do you want people to trust what you say, but you also want them to trust you to make decisions because they believe in your word.

For instance, if you are too optimistic about someone, people might think you have a positive bias towards that individual and can't see any blind spots. This can hurt your chances of supporting someone who's worth it.

On the flip side, if you are always pessimistic about someone, they might think you have a negative bias towards that individual and can't see the positive qualities they have.

You want to be balanced in your communication. Think duality, think yin and yang. If you can articulate the pros and cons of people and things, and use the right pitch and tone to emphasize your most important points, people are more likely to believe what you are saying.

In this chapter, we'll cover several points that can make or break your communication. But the first and most important point I need you to understand is this:

Be careful with what you say, because you can guarantee it's being taken literally.

I once told a store manager early in my career as a district manager that "I better not see any back stock" the next time I visit your store. Guess what happened? I didn't see any back stock. I was quite impressed, blown away, and a little surprised, actually, because this was a very high dollar per square foot location—we're talking about $1000 per square foot. We had a great full-day visit, and I flew home that night.

I woke up to a voicemail in the morning from the mall manager. They let me know they had the store manager on camera using rolling racks to move product from the backroom into a U-Haul. Yup, you guessed it. This is how they had no back stock for the day of the visit.

Now, what this person did was unacceptable. However, what I said in my previous visit was too literal and created unrealistic expectations. This particular leader, rather than owning up to what he could or couldn't deliver, simply tried to deliver it, albeit unethically.

As leaders, we have to own our communication. Make sure you're not giving anyone room to misinterpret you.

Nothing is ever "always" or "never". Nothing is all or nothing. People tend to exaggerate the truth when trying to make a point, and it only gets in the way of someone's ability to believe them. When I hear someone say "always" or "never", I immediately stop them and ask, "So you always listen?", "You always clean up after yourself?", or "You have never been late?", "You have never made a mistake?"

When people use extreme words like "always" and "never", they are trying to achieve something with their communication rather than just stating the facts. There's a big difference.

Early in my career, I was the king of this kind of extreme language. I communicated to get things so well for quite some time that I was able to achieve a lot. Make sure you don't come off like a bullshit artist, and make sure to sniff out those who do around you.

They may not be a bad person, or even doing it on purpose; they just might not know any different. I didn't until I was about 20 years old. I just needed someone to call me out on my exaggerations (thank you, Dave Temple) and be given the opportunity to course correct.

With that said, here's a breakdown of every communication practice you need to master to level up.

SAY IT RIGHT AWAY

Have you ever told yourself, "I'll tell them the next time I see them," then when you do see them, something gets in the way and you think, "I'll tell them next time," but then it never gets said?

Some of you might do this unintentionally, really planning to tell them next time. Others might do it intentionally, to avoid conflict or even giving praise.

That's why you need a 24-hour rule. Sure, there are exceptions, but missing the 24-hour window should be rare. Why? Because when something that needs to be said remains unsaid, it slows down progress for everyone. It's crucial input that someone needs to either improve on an opportunity or reinforce a strength.

The best chance of success comes from saying it in the moment. Your chances decrease if you miss this window, but they're still better if you say it within 24 hours. The longer you wait to say it, the lower your chances of achieving what you intended with your words.

If you haven't been doing this in your career so far, don't just switch gears without warning. Let those you regularly communicate with know about this change and why you're making it. Explain that it might be different from how you've communicated before, but it will help everyone, including yourself, grow faster.

If you don't let people know about this shift in your approach ahead of time, many won't know how to react. They'll find your new way of communicating out of character.

If you are a great leader, you often have what may be perceived as tough conversations. It's important to remember to observe how people receive communication for clues as to whether it's a tough conversation or not. This is because it's tough if they perceive it that way, not if you determine it to be on your end.

If you observe or think something might have been perceived as a tough conversation, it's important to check back in on them within 24 hours, and preferably before the end of the day itself or first thing in the morning.

Following up or checking back in, asking the person how they are doing, how they handled the feedback, and letting them know that you want them to benefit from it and not the other way around is important.

This gives you the opportunity to have many more of these tough conversations in the future, and the more of these you can have freely, the faster you can progress people.

CLARIFYING

Think about the last thing you needed from someone and

think of the steps you took to communicate that need. Did you use the least amount of words possible to get your point across? Did you explain how the work would benefit them, their team and the organization? Did you take 3 to 4 times the amount of time preparing what to say as you actually said it? Was this what you talked about first, most and last in your conversation?

If you did, kudos. My guess is your communication landed nicely. If you didn't, my guess is you still don't have what you need from this person.

Like with everything we talk about in this book, it's all about increasing our odds of success as either an employee or leader. Nothing is ever guaranteed, other than certain things will guarantee to increase the odds.

Words matter and so does contribution. If you say the exact right words and spend the appropriate amount of time on the subject, the word and the time will resonate.

HEARING VS LISTENING

"There is a difference between hearing and listening," said Wesley Snipes in White Men Can't Jump. His character Sidney Deane went on to deliver some comedic relief after this line, but there's truth to the statement.

You might be listening, but are you really hearing what's being said? That's the crucial part. You need to stop your internal chatter and give the person talking the respect they deserve.

When you quiet your own thoughts, you can actually hear the words being spoken. You can notice the pitch and tone of their voice and observe their body language. Paying attention to the words, pitch, tone, and body language gives you the best chance of understanding what's truly being said, even if it's different from the actual words.

Here's an example. Imagine your spouse slams their finger in a door and shouts, "Damn it!" You ask if they're okay, and they yell back, "YES, I'M FINE." What they said isn't really what you should be hearing.

If you only consider two of these inputs—like just the words and tone—your chances of really understanding drop. And if you focus on just one, like only the words, then you're far less likely to grasp the true message.

REFLECTING AND COMMITTING

Your chances of actually hearing what is being said increase when you listen to the words, understand the pitch and tone, and observe the body language. But even then, you're not guaranteed 100% accuracy.

This is where reflective listening comes in. To make sure you've completely understood the other person, you should repeat back what they said, as you interpreted it. For example, "So, you're saying you're not okay, and your finger hurts? Can I help?"

Many leaders just say their piece and think that's enough. They believe that once they've communicated—whether through email, a conference call, or in person—their job is done. Now the responsibility is on others.

Back in the Blackberry era, I was shadowing a new district manager. Over a couple of days, we hit up six or seven stores, but none of the improvements he'd promised were in place. He was both surprised and annoyed, constantly muttering, "Why aren't they following my instructions?"

He believed his Monday emails should have been enough; he was relying entirely on mass emails for communication. He overlooked the essential elements of interaction and the opportunity for feedback.

I decided it was time for a drastic measure: I took away his Blackberry and banned him from email for a month.

He had no choice but to directly talk to his team. This shift forced him to improve his communication skills significantly, turning him into an effective communicator.

Ask yourself this: As a leader or coach, how often have you had to repeat instructions to someone? Chances are, it's happened quite a lot. This usually occurs because you don't ask the people you're communicating with to reflect on what they heard. If they repeat back exactly what you said, great, there's mutual understanding. If not, you can correct any misunderstandings on the spot.

Now, from an employee's perspective, think about when you've misunderstood directions or accepted more work than was realistic, leading to unmet commitments. This is where you need to use the accountability skills from Pillar One. Reflect back what you're hearing to your boss to ensure alignment and commitment. Also, internally assess if the request is realistic before committing.

For example, you might clarify, "Just to confirm, next week you want me to spend 50% of my time helping my peers with visual merchandising and the other 50% on recruiting?" Your boss might clarify, saying they only need two days for visual merchandising, leaving the rest of the week to your discretion.

Or, if you're worried about unrealistic expectations, you could say, "I'm hesitant to commit to completing these five tasks by next Friday. I'm more comfortable with these three by then, and the other two the following week, and here's why." Your boss might agree or discuss why they think all five are doable.

The key is using reflective listening to ensure both you and your team are focused on the right tasks, boosting your chances of success as close to 100% as possible.

THE 3 STRIKE RULE

I believe in a three-strike rule when it comes to developing talent. The first time you don't do something, maybe it was my miscommunication. The second time you don't do the same thing, I'll give you the benefit of the doubt, maybe again it was my miscommunication. The third time, even if it was my miscommunication, I have at least attempted two other times to communicate the need differently and they still aren't doing it. This is when I shift to documentation or something more severe to try to get a change in behavior. This three-strike rule really helps me be sure the miss isn't my fault. However, at some point, and the third strike usually occurs pretty quickly if you are an attentive leader, if they aren't going to do the work, it gets addressed.

This is why when someone doesn't do something a third time, I present them with the issue and only give them one example at a time. If they agree with the incorrect behavior after the first example, I don't even bring up the second or third because they are unnecessary. If they don't agree after the first or second example and I have to bring up the third example, I know that they aren't likely going to change their behavior and, along with documentation, I start to succession plan as well.

This is why reflective communication is so important. When you reflect back what you hear from others in your own words, it gives the other person the chance to agree or correct what we heard. As leaders, we must ask those we communicate with to reflect back what they heard in their words as well to ensure they understood what we wanted them to hear. (This ties back to the "White Men Can't Jump" commentary in the book). Reflecting in the moment will save you thousands of hours over the course of your career.

ASSUME THE BEST INTENTIONS—AND REWARD THEM IMMEDIATELY

Assume people did the right thing and let them say or feel otherwise.

Stop assuming people didn't do what you asked or what the company asked them to do. Many of us do this. We walk up to someone and ask, "Did you stock the newest product up front?" or "Did you complete the final step in the project yet?"

Talking this way puts the recipient on the defensive. In the best case, they did what you're asking about and get frustrated for being questioned. In the worst case, they become defensive and blame you for not trusting them.

When you change your language to assume they did what

they were supposed to, a lot changes for the better.

Instead of asking, "Did you stock the newest product up front?" you can say, "Was it difficult to stock the newest product up front this morning when the shipment arrived?" This way, you're assuming they did it, and they can either appreciate your trust and explain how it went, or they have to admit they didn't do it. In this case, they might feel like they let you down, someone who obviously trusted them to do what they were asked, instead of feeling defensive because they were being questioned.

Then, when you do notice excellence, hand out praise quickly and eagerly. When you enter a store, review a project, or engage in a conversation, look for what's right before seeing what's wrong. You'll be amazed at what you find. And if you aren't proactive and intentional in looking for what people are doing great at, you might miss the chance to recognize it.

When you recognize behaviors, they are more likely to be replicated. If you miss opportunities to recognize behaviors, there's a great chance they'll stop doing them altogether.

Trust me, don't worry about not finding the opportunities or the time to critique. You'll find plenty. This approach just makes sure you see what you want replicated and have the time to discuss it with them.

I remember in my first few years as a Regional Director, my 360 feedback reviews would come back with really high marks in all categories except one: recognition. My team was very blunt in saying that I didn't give it. I was flabbergasted when I saw the feedback. I asked my team questions and also looked in the mirror, realizing that the way I recognized folks was either by giving them more work because they were doing well, or by spending more time with them and therefore finding more opportunities for them to work on. My intentions were good, but my output wasn't.

I shifted to catching people doing things right to ensure I was looking for it, and also created space to share my findings with the teams.

This approach not only helps you develop people more effectively, but it also creates greater trust and appreciation for you as a leader, and you will gain more followers. By gaining more followers, you will have more people to communicate with and influence.

PERFORMANCE MANAGEMENT

This approach is different from the 'see it, say it' moments. It refers to conversations needed after observing someone's performance over time. If you're good at those immediate 'see it, say it' moments, you'll have fewer of these longer-term discussions because people will regularly know how they're doing.

Performance management often feels like it's just about

correcting performance, which can bring up negative emotions. That's why many people avoid it. They don't like conflict and justify not having these conversations, saying it's easier for the other person, when in reality, they're avoiding it because it's easier for themselves.

In my first few months as a District Manager, I quickly learned that tough conversations were part of the job. To handle this, I developed a strategy to make sure I followed through. I kept my boss in the loop about what was going on and what I planned to do, down to the exact days I intended to have those difficult talks. This approach of having someone hold me accountable was invaluable in the beginning, even though I eventually grew out of needing it—and you'll need to learn to hold yourself accountable if you want to level up.

The truth is, performance management is about effectively managing performance, which involves communicating both what needs to change and what should continue.

For an employee or team player, managing your own performance is key to success. So, why not have that inner dialogue with yourself about areas for improvement or achievements worth recognizing?

As a leader or coach, managing others' performance is also crucial. You won't win many games if your team's performance isn't managed daily. By not discussing both the good and the bad, you're holding back those you're responsible for. They won't know what to improve or what to keep doing.

Do your homework and have examples to back up your conversation. I recommend having three examples to support a strength or an area of improvement. Having three examples for a positive behavior you want to acknowledge and see more of ensures it's a consistent behavior contributing to something bigger.

Three examples for a negative behavior lend credibility to your words. The key is not to present all three at once. Start with one example. If they agree, you can align on an action plan and move on. If not, bring up the second example and pause, allowing for uncomfortable silence, which is a great skill to master. If they still don't agree after the second example, present the third and pause again. Why three examples? Because if they don't see the issue after three, they're unlikely to, and you have a bigger problem. That's when you don't need a fourth example. Agree to disagree, communicate what needs to change, and move on.

To have the best chance of understanding what is really being said, pay attention to the words, pitch, tone, and body language.

Teach yourself, your employees, and your team members to reflect back on what they hear. This practice ensures everyone commits to the right tasks and feels confident about the associated timelines.

PRO TIP FOR MULTI-STORE FIELD LEADERS: MAKE UNANNOUNCED VISITS

Try not to announce you're visiting a store ahead of time. Why? Because you need to experience what the customer experiences to really understand how your team serves them. Also, people will put on a show when they know you're coming. They might spend more payroll than they're allowed or get help from neighboring stores. You'll see a beautiful store but won't actually help the team. Our job is to identify performance gaps and help teams improve them. An unannounced visit will tell you almost everything you need to know.

How to visit most of the time without giving a "gotcha" feeling? When you look to give out praise and catch people doing things right, you'll be able to point out good things. Praise during an unannounced visit feels great because it's genuine. Sure, you might find more issues, but now you know what they are and can help the team close the gap, improving the customer experience.

If you notice the same problems in multiple locations, first look at yourself and your company. It's likely that you or the company are the obstacles. If it's an issue in a few stores but not most, it's likely the leaders of those stores need help.

I really learned this approach from my wife, who used to work in retail. As a district manager, she would visit 95% of the time unannounced. She would make many visits with the general manager off to see how their support team performed and how knowledgeable they were. She used this approach to gauge how well general managers were developing their talent and communicating with them.

Unannounced visits are hard for the person doing them because they have to face the truth directly, and many leaders don't want to do that. But the truth is where the hard work is. It requires you to look in the mirror first before looking at others. However, when you do the hard work, you progress not only those you are accountable to (employees and customers) but also yourself.

MAKING THE SHIFT

I remember when I committed to my own communication shift. It was during my second stint as a Store Manager at the Santa Anita Mall, working for Pacific Sunwear of California in the mid-90s. I noticed something in my two assistant managers at the time, Helen and Liza. They had tremendous potential and were so receptive to feedback that it made the 'see it, say it' approach easy for me.

Both Helen and Liza went on to run their own stores and performed exceptionally well. This experience was my first real taste of what it feels like to prioritize development.

I was hooked and found my purpose nearly 30 years ago, thanks to these two women, and I've never looked back. Over the next 30 years or so, not everyone was as open to a 'see it, say it' approach. At times, I found myself either avoiding conflict or being too busy in the moment to give feedback. One thing was certain: whenever I avoided conflict or was too busy, my business suffered, and no one on my team grew.

My advice to all retail leaders is this: when you see something that needs correcting or deserves praise, care enough about your team to tell them.

I once had a boss who said to me, "I can develop you in the way you might prefer, which means I will have to think about everything I say when I say it, to ensure it's most appropriate for your learning style. Or I can develop you my way, which may be more painful and feel a bit like the growing pains you had as a kid. This is because I won't think before I speak; I will simply tell you what I'm observing so you can get a lot more information in a shorter period of time. You just need to tell me which you would prefer. I'm good with either approach."

I, of course, said I would prefer it the hard way. It sure was hard, but I was thrown the kitchen sink and able to take in a ton in a very short period of time, which helped propel me to a Regional Director at the age of 25. I have since adopted this question and used it with many people who have worked with me in the following years.

Interestingly enough, I only had one person actually tell me they would prefer it the easy way...you can guess how that worked out!

CHAPTER EIGHT

INFLUENCE

Once you have strengthened your developmental and basic communication skills it's time to shift to your influential skills. This is where you are able to really multiply your results for your efforts. When you can influence folks, you will be able to further develop folks and also communicate with that much of a greater ROI.

You won't be able to influence others however until you have a respect for your own tendencies. Once you have that, you will respect the tendencies of others and acknowledge and embrace them as they are and therefore find greater solutions on how to move yourself and others forward.

PERSONALITY

I remember it like it was yesterday. I read the book "The Platinum Rule," took the test, and came out as a 'Thinking

Socializer.' Reading the description, I was frustrated, even though it clearly matched my personality. I couldn't help but compare my type to the 'Director' personality. I thought to myself, "I'll never be the Michael Jordan of retail; he obviously has a director personality."

I didn't really pay attention to organized personality types until I was a few years into being a district manager. Before this, I led based on instinct and observation, but I couldn't describe what I now know in such detail.

I immediately dove into understanding how and why people tick the way they do. I read about their strengths, opportunities, triggers, and tried my best to lead them according to the personality styles described in the book. Since "The Platinum Rule," I've read hundreds of articles and books on the subject, and they all say similar things in different ways.

When I retested and came out as a 'Socializing Director,' I realized that my circumstances influenced how I answered the questions, slightly shifting my personality test results. In a comfortable job or role, I always test as a 'Thinking Socializer,' which is about a 7 out of 10 on the assertiveness scale and a 6 out of 10 on the responsiveness scale. When stressed or needing to lead more assertively, I tend to test more like a director, scoring a 9 or 10 (out of 10) in assertiveness, and only around a 3 in responsiveness.

At some point, I shifted my focus from reading others

to truly understanding myself. Only after I recognized and respected my superpowers and areas of opportunity, could I truly respect and understand others' styles. For example, when working with a highly assertive but minimally responsive leader, I learned to respect their style as I did my own. These types of people typically need freedom to feel good, but require guardrails. If you don't provide them freedom, they will feel disrespected and produce less. If you don't provide guardrails, however, they won't respect you and they will run all over you.

This is important because once you respect your own style and others', you can truly influence people's actions and behaviors by communicating in an appropriate, real, and authentic way.

"Strengths-Based Leadership" is similar to personality style books, but my challenge with this philosophy is that many people focus only on their strengths. While leveraging strengths is important for development and work, ignoring blind spots, areas of opportunity, and triggers can be problematic. Not recognizing when you're acting out of character or helping others who are stuck can hinder progress.

ARE PERSONALITIES SET IN STONE?

The majority of your personality may be fixed, but you can adapt. It starts with respecting your own tendencies and understanding its strengths and opportunities. This way, you aren't judging and shaming your personality; you're leveraging it and learning from it.

I mentioned that when you are stressed, you might answer some questions on a personality test a little differently. This is because stress may cause you to act a bit out of character. This isn't always a bad thing because the situation might require you to. It's important to understand that the majority of your personality may be static, but that's not the entire you.

Many people and organizations would like you to think that by a certain age, you are who you are. So much so that they have you take tests and determine if they should hire you based on what the test predicts about your personality, rather than what the hiring manager senses based on his or her experience.

I get it, and I know these tests help minimize the risk of a hire, and because of that, I understand why they are used. That said, like any analytical approach, it should be counterbalanced with the human approach. Yet again, this is where respect for duality comes into play.

You may be an introvert. You may be an extrovert. You may also flex out of either of these personalities because a situation arises. The key here is to respect the personality that is you and understand when it advantages or disadvantages you.

We know a growth mindset works and fixed mindsets don't. If you believe your personality is static, it's no different than having a fixed mindset. You will believe you are who you are, where you are, and there's nothing you can do about it. Not true.

SELFISHNESS

I loved Simon Sinek's TED Talk about finding your 'why.' It brilliantly explained why businesses succeed and fail. I struggled to understand my own 'why,' which bothered me a lot. It wasn't until I realized that everyone, including myself, is selfish, that things started to make sense. So, what does being selfish have to do with my 'why'? It turns out, being selfish is the 'why.' What we are selfish about drives our passion and productivity.

For me, it's about being part of someone's development

THE RETAIL LEADER'S ROADMAP

and growth. Knowing that my role matters in another person's journey is what gets me going. I feel this way about my bosses, the people I lead, and my peers. When they grow because of something I did, that's my fuel.

I have found that the flipside is also true. If my boss can't learn from me, I have a hard time working for them. The more open people are around me to learning from me, the more fuel I have and want to give them.

In leadership, it's important to understand your own selfishness and how to feed it while still being a good citizen.

I had someone work for me who was extremely charitable. She dedicated hours to supporting others. She was selfish, too. These acts were her 'why,' her fuel. Her actions, driven by selfishness, benefited many others! Her empathy, which could be seen as a weakness, is actually a superpower that can greatly boost productivity.

I've also worked with people who needed to be #1 at all costs. They were selfish in their pursuit of winning because it was their fuel. Their selfishness could be beneficial if understood correctly.

Once you understand and respect your selfishness, instead of feeling ashamed or unaware of it, you can leverage it and understand others' selfishness too. You won't get defensive about others' tendencies and can learn to meet people where their 'why' is, fueling them to drive the business in new ways.

Now that you get that you are selfish, respect it and know you can use this power for good. When you see others' selfish tendencies, grant them grace and show interest in what they genuinely care about.

When people understand that doing great work and being appreciated for it fulfills them, they'll go to great lengths for you as a leader, peer, or employee.

Understanding that someone's need to be #1 isn't bad, but just a characteristic, means you won't be defensive. By acknowledging and embracing this reality, you can work with them to find ways to win at the right costs.

EGO

Ego by definition is the defense of your self concept. Over time you have created a view of yourself and whenever this view is threatened the dreaded ego goes to work. It's your defense mechanism for protection and although the ego's job is meant to keep you safe, it actually keeps you from evolving.

One of the many ways it shows itself is when you don't understand something. If you don't understand it, it must not be understandable, because if it were and you didn't understand it, it must mean you are inferior. This is how the mind can play tricks on you.

Another way it shows up is when you see a behavior in

someone else that you don't possess. An example might be when you see someone who's glass is always half full. If your glass tends to be half empty all the time, you see the negative in the other person because it makes you feel better about your way of thinking.

Being defensive is what the ego does and its job is to keep you safe. Comfortable is safe. If you don't try new things or look for new perspectives, you are safe.

Here's an example from my own career: three months into having a new boss, it was clear that neither of us was really connecting with the other. We both weren't making much effort to meet halfway.

One night, while I was venting my frustration, my wife gave me some straightforward advice. She told me to find the professional contribution my boss had to offer and meet him where he was. Alternatively, I should look for a job elsewhere because my boss, or any boss for that matter, wouldn't be the one to make the first move.

So, I followed her advice. I recognized a valuable contribution from my boss and made the effort to meet him 75% of the way. Once I did that, I found that he reciprocated, and I started getting what I needed from the relationship too. The key difference here was letting go of my ego first, instead of waiting for him to let go of his. In the end, we both ended up lowering our guards and egos multiple times in front of each other, which led to a much healthier working relationship for both of us.

Ego is not necessarily a bad thing. It sure can be, but it doesn't have to be. The key is to recognize it and be in control of it, not the other way around. Ego can actually fuel you rather than stall you out if used appropriately. I have found that I am in my happy place when I am comfortable with my ego.

I wear black, ride Harley Davidsons, drive Ford F-150s, have tattoos, work out, run, etc. When I am either wearing black, driving my Ford, in a tattoo shop, or out for a run, I feel my best. I stand tall or walk with a strut. What's wrong with that? I simply feel good about myself in that moment. This should be expressed outwardly.

The problem is most people take themselves too seriously, and this is where the danger comes into play.

For example, if I took myself too seriously, I would look down on those who wear bright colors, ride Kawasakis, drive Chevys, have no tattoos, or don't work out. I would not be respectful of the duality that is life.

It's still fair for me to stand tall and walk with a strut when I am in my element, but it's not fair for me to look down on others or feel less than when I am out of my element. I have to find ways to walk as tall and with a strut even when I am in a rental car that happens to be a Prius. I like to channel John Travolta in Get Shorty, when he continually refers to his Oldsmobile Silhouette as "the Cadillac of minivans". Intentional swagger has its place!

Like everything else, it's how you manage it. If you let ego run you, it's bad. If you run the ego, it's good.

So, stop listening to all the negative talk around ego and start understanding it. Do your homework.

EMOTIONS

Managing emotions, I've found, is all about intentionality.

If you are emotionally reactive:

You aren't in control of your mind and therefore your past is running the show. Your Ego is defending you because of the image you have created of yourself over the years. Your Ego is in control and you are simply falling in line.

Whereas if you are intentionally emotional:

Your mind is in complete control and you are using emotion to create a particular response in someone else.

In the movie "Air," which is about Michael Jordan's shoe contract with Nike, Sonny, the key person behind the deal, mentioned to a business partner that he needed to get Phil Knight, the creator of Nike, angry and scared. At first, this didn't make sense, but later in the movie, after Sonny intentionally upset and frightened Phil, Phil agreed with Sonny's proposal and took a risk with his board members, reminiscent of Nike's early days.

You might think that always being in control of your emotions turns you into a robot. For many, including myself, emotions have been key to success. I'm high-energy and passionate. Learning to harness this energy was crucial. Sometimes I was amped up, but deliberately, knowing it would elicit the response needed from someone else to achieve a particular result.

Emotions are discussed late in this book because for most people, managing them is the hardest skill to develop. You can reach great heights even if you don't fully control your emotions, especially if they're directly tied to your field. Most retailers are high-energy, and emotional reactions often fit in well, until they don't.

Consider the leader who reacts to everything and ends up diminishing the importance of everything, leading to people tuning out. Or the leader who takes work stress home, becomes angry with loved ones, and ends up resenting their job.

Emotions can be tricky as they're often part of our DNA. If we are a certain way most of the time, we might defend it if someone says it's unacceptable, as it's part of our identity.

That's why working on your own emotions is key. It's easier to accept feedback from yourself than from others, and you're less likely to be defensive, though your ego might try to interfere.

I recall being called into my Human Resource Director's office when I was a new Regional Director. She told me to slow down my communication and expectations because my team couldn't keep up. I took offense and insisted that they had to keep up with me.

It was only years later that I realized I reacted emotionally because I felt my personality was being attacked. My speed had been a key factor in my career success.

If you challenge someone's emotions, they'll likely get defensive. To effectively coach someone, you can't let their ego be a barrier. I would advise the HR Director to acknowledge my natural high energy and quick pace, then suggest learning to create pause moments in conversations for reflection and understanding.

The most important takeaway on emotions: stay present.

The quickest way to spin your emotions out of control is to wish things were different than they are.

I have found that in each moment you are wishing something were different, you invite anxiety and or anger into play.

I wish I had a different car, made more money, my son's attitude was different, a particular person would respond differently to me, and so on and so on.

When you are anxious and or angry, it's almost impossible to think clearly and find solutions to anything. People tend to act impulsively.

Just think about it, how can you be happy when you wish things were different? It's impossible because you are telling yourself that what you have is insufficient.

Christian Conte writes:

> There is a difference between what I call the cartoon
> world and the real world. The cartoon world is the
> world as you demand it to be; the real world, on the
> other hand, is the world as it is. One reflects your imagi-
> nation, whereas the other reflects reality. The more you
> align your expectations with your cartoon world, the
> more you feel let down, but the truth is the world isn't
> letting you down, because the world is simply what it is.
> Instead, you are the one who is letting yourself down,
> because you are expecting the world to be something
> it isn't.

BLEND CONFIDENCE AND HUMILITY

If you want others to be influenced by you, they need to see
you as confident and as someone who can help them.

When you are not competing, that's where humility belongs.
This is when you are curious and looking for ways to improve.
When you are competing, that's where confidence comes in.
You act as though you have been here before because, in many
ways, you have. You have learned and prepared for it.

Doubting your capabilities at this point will do you no good.

Now, if you didn't prepare and weren't humble enough to learn, your confidence will come off as arrogance because you won't have put in the real work.

I used to think I lacked humility and was overconfident early in my career, up until I was 30 years old. In hindsight, I learned that wasn't the case. I actually had a great balance of the two. I was curious, wanted to learn, and was open to feedback.

I appeared more confident than humble to either myself or maybe even others because I was competing most of my time. I was working to be better than the day before and at the same time be number one at whatever I found most important.

I also worked on myself a ton when I was competing, early mornings or late evenings. Nobody saw that side of me. It was happening while others were sleeping or out partying.

Later in my career, I found myself thinking I needed to be more humble. Maybe it was appearing more humble when in fact I was really humble all along.

I also found that I had less time to work on myself outside of work, so I had to do it during the day job. This meant when I was supposed to be competing, I was practicing too. My humility was now more on display for others to see, and like with all things duality, if you see humility, you might not see as much confidence and vice versa.

It wasn't until very recently that I recognized my early observations were incorrect. You can be both humble and confident. You don't need to act out either one. This is where the "don't fake it until you make it" comment fails you.

Be curious, learn, respect duality, and understand that yes, you may be right, but someone else may be more "righter"! Put in the practice so when it's game time (which is the majority of the day job), you are exuding confidence.

DON'T TAKE ANYTHING PERSONALLY

I remember working for someone who was so deathly afraid of looking bad that they hovered over everyone's shoulders. It wasn't that they didn't trust you; it was that they couldn't trust you because, God forbid, you did something that might make them look bad.

I remember working for someone who used to tell me not to space the clothing on hangers just because it made it look better and to focus on sizing it instead. When I told them I was doing both, they said it was a waste of time and unnecessary.

These examples are about their insecurities and not your capabilities. In one instance, it was because one person was afraid of looking bad, and in the other instance, it was because they looked down on people who had too much flair.

Nine out of ten times, people's reactions to you have nothing to do with you. It has everything to do with their ego and past experiences.

If we receive a negative reaction to something, we need to

put forth more effort to understand where they are coming from to be in the driver's seat to increase your odds of getting what you want out of it.

LEVEL UP

This is about a topic many of you might not like discussing.

If you work for someone else, they largely control your progression and, in turn, your ability to progress others. This is true even if you don't work for someone else, as your customer then becomes the one you work for, and they too control your progression.

So you need to meet your boss, and their boss, a minimum of 51% of the way.

If you're not aligned with your boss, and they're not aligned with you, you're stuck. The same goes if you're not aligned with their boss. Your boss needs you to actively support their agenda, and their boss needs to see your value in potentially working for them and driving their agenda.

I've worked with leaders who appreciate debate and see a difference of opinion as a strength. They often support more combative leaders and get frustrated with those who always agree and avoid conflict. I've also worked with leaders who prefer followers and executors. These leaders keep to themselves, do what they're told, and rarely debate with the boss, viewing it as disrespectful.

FIND YOUR PROFESSIONAL CONTRIBUTION

Have you ever been told to get out of your own way? I have—both said it and heard it. In this chapter, we've talked about personalities, selfishness, ego, and emotions. These personal tendencies often obstruct us and our leaders.

The better we understand and accept these tendencies as just that—tendencies shaped by people's pasts and defensiveness—the more we can see what a person truly offers.

We need to look beyond someone's style or approach. Some are soft-spoken, others abrasive.

We need to understand people's selfish tendencies, what makes them feel good. For some, it's charity, for others, it's winning a gold medal.

We need to see past when someone is defensive or adamant about their point of view. To them, it's either black or white, right or wrong.

We need to understand emotional reactions. Some see crying as weakness, others see directness as meanness.

The key is not to label someone by these traits but to understand why they appear, offer grace, and see beyond them.

FOLLOWERSHIP

For many, the concept of followership contradicts what we've been taught since childhood: to be leaders, not followers. But being a good follower is crucial in everyone's journey. Following the right people can skyrocket your career, while following the wrong ones can stall it, or kill it altogether.

But you also need to know when not to follow—in other words, you need to recognize when it's time to leave.

You should leave when you realize you can't or won't meet your boss or their boss halfway and when you can't find a professional contribution in them. If you don't make this decision, they will, either by firing you for performance, through an organizational restructure, or in other ways. If you don't lose your job, you'll still feel lost, losing sleep and unable to enjoy time with friends and family.

One way or another, if you don't leave, they will make the decision for you.

PILLAR TWO WRAP-UP

Building connections starts with yourself. You have to do the work to understand your own personality, ego, selfishness, and emotions. Look inward before you look outward to influence others.

The significance of building connections for retail leaders can't be overstated; other people play a crucial role in your journey toward success. Despite your efforts and talents, your achievements often depend on the relationships you cultivate and the networks you develop.

You can't control other people's actions or decisions—however, this realization should not lead to sitting back and letting things "happen to you". Take ownership. Developing relationships means investing time and effort to understand the people in your professional circle, recognizing their strengths, interests, and motivations.

While you may not have complete control over how others impact your journey, you have the tools to build connections that can significantly enhance your path to success. By focusing on developing, communicating, and influencing, you can create a supportive network that propels you toward your goals.

Ask yourself these five questions:

1. Can I Hire, Promote and Retain people more effectively?
   (Or am I already getting it right 90% of the time?)

2. Can I catch more people doing things right?

3. Can I be more timely with my feedback?

4. Can I be more appreciative of everyone's personality,
   selfishness, ego, and emotions (inclusive of my own?)

5. Can I meet my boss and their boss 51% of the way?

PILLAR THREE

BUILD YOUR PLAN

A PLAN IS A DETAILED PROPOSAL FOR DOING OR ACHIEVING SOMETHING. THIS IS WHERE YOU PUT PEN TO PAPER AND WORDS AND THOUGHTS INTO ACTION. THIS IS WHERE YOU DELIVER ON YOUR CRAFT AND CAPABILITIES.

IF YOU WANT TO DELIVER ON YOUR CRAFT AND CAPABILITIES, YOU WILL NEED TO DO WHAT 80% OF THE POPULATION THAT SURROUNDS YOU WON'T DO.

YOUR CAREER IS A SERIES OF SPRINTS, NOT A MARATHON.

CHAPTER NINE

EARN WHILE YOU LEARN

Before planning for your future, remember that your retail education, like university, costs money. It's important to earn while you learn.

Your performance in your day job justifies your salary and gives you the chance to learn. When you perform well, people often give you the benefit of the doubt, believing you know what you're doing, and usually leave you to your own devices. However, as mentioned in the "Build your Connections Pillar," leaders shouldn't always take this approach. Be aware, leaders tend to closely monitor those who underperform. If you're in this group, every mistake is scrutinized, leaving little room for learning from them.

So, the first step is to excel in your day job. Aim to be at least in the top three in everything you do—I call this "making it to the podium". Consistently being among the best puts you in line for recognition and more responsibility, leading to further education and growth.

This ties into balancing humility and confidence. Be humble while practicing and confident while competing. Adequate practice leads to plenty of humility. Moreover, with enough practice, confidence naturally builds, readying you for game time.

I recently came across a quote that struck a chord with me, especially when thinking about balancing humility and confidence:

"Practice like you've never won, and play the game like you've never lost."

It's about being vulnerable yet walking tall with confidence, something people admire and follow.

But is just performing well in your day job enough to climb the ladder? Not really. You could be a top salesperson raking in commissions, a brilliant merchant, or even an outstanding Store Manager, District Manager, or Regional Director, but that doesn't necessarily mean you're cut out for the next level.

It's about not just performing well but also showing potential. You need to excel in your current role while also demonstrating the ability to take on more and make a bigger impact on people and businesses.

So, how do you do both at the same time?

You excel in your day job by focusing on what I call the 5 P's of Performance:

1. People

2. Product

3. Priorities

4. Processes

5. Productivity

You prove your potential to impact more people and businesses by consistently improving your character and connections.

Since you need to earn to learn, let's dive into the 5 P's of performance. This plan is divided into Steps, which are subdivided into Actions. I want to make it as simple and straightforward as possible for you to implement this into your day-to-day routines; you're busy enough as it is.

STEP 1: PEOPLE ANALYSIS

ACTION 1: RANK YOUR REPORTS

First, if you have direct reports, rank them in order of importance. If you're working solo, you can skip straight to focusing on the product.

The aim is to optimize your team. You need the right people in the right roles at the right times. Start by assigning your top performer to the most crucial tasks. Then, work to improve your weakest team member until they're better than the best of your competitors. Being optimal lets you be proactive, not reactive, in leadership.

Why rank your team? Because performance and capability vary greatly among individuals. To know where to focus your efforts, you need a clear picture of your team's current state.

Think of it like a sports draft or choosing teams during school recess. You always picked the best player available. Start by asking yourself, "Who is the one person I absolutely need on my team?" This person is your top pick.

Deciding who's indispensable requires short-term and long-term thinking. It could be your current top performer, or someone with the potential to excel in the future—like a promising minor league player who's bound to make it big.

It might also be someone in a crucial role, without whom

EARN WHILE YOU LEARN

you'd struggle. This could be someone managing a remote area with no backup, or a team member with unique expertise that's vital for your operations.

Refer to the Character and Connection Practices outlined in the first two pillars of the book for guidance, as these qualities are timeless.

Force ranking involves more than just current performance. It's about evaluating who is most to least critical to your team's success now and in the future.

I know it's tough to label someone as the least important, but it's a necessary reality in leadership. Acknowledging and accepting this helps you become the coach your entire team needs to succeed.

ACTION 2: CREATE IMPROVEMENT PLANS

Next, you need to ponder two crucial questions:

1. For each direct report, identify one or two specific behaviors or skills they lack compared to the person ranked just above them in your force rank. Which of these skills, if developed, could help them move up in the ranking next quarter?

2. What do others in your professional circle need from you in the coming quarter? This includes peers,

business partners, bosses, etc.

Many companies have a set of competencies they value in their employees. You can use these as a reference to pinpoint the one or two areas each team member needs to work on. You can also draw from the character and connection practices discussed in this book, or simply go with your own observations.

For instance, a team member might need to enhance their talent-building skills, a typical company competency. Or, they might need to improve their communication skills, as detailed in this book. Sometimes, it's as simple as noticing that someone needs to talk less and listen more, a skill not always found in textbooks.

Why focus on just one or two behaviors or skills? And why compare each person to the one ranked above them? Most leaders are focused on developing individuals rather than the whole team. But if you're a leader, you're responsible for developing the entire team as a unit, not just as a collection of individuals. This approach levels up your entire team at once while individuals are developed, which is transformative. It's about consistently improving performance quarter by quarter, faster than anyone else.

Here's an example. Imagine your second-most valuable direct report needs to be more proactive and less reliant on asking for permission to surpass the top-ranked individual.

Over the next 90 days, guided by your feedback and influence, they start showing these behaviors. There's a good chance that in three months, you might find it harder not to rank them at the top.

In the worst-case scenario, which is still positive, both your top two direct reports exceed expectations, strengthening your top 20% and, consequently, your entire team.

Many people focus only on improving their weakest performers. Some consider both the top and bottom, but few pay attention to those in the middle. By identifying specific improvement areas for each team member, you uplift the entire team. Also, by identifying the 1 to 2 things each person can improve on, and communicating them effectively, each person can work on themselves, too.

Now that you know who your most and least valuable team members are, and what each needs to improve, it's time to consider what everyone else in your professional sphere needs from you.

Why is this important? As discussed in the 'Building Your Connections' section, relationships involve give and take. If you're in a relationship with someone, it's crucial to first consider what you can offer them.

Don't just guess what they need; ask them directly. "What specific support can I provide this quarter that would most benefit your success?" Ensure you understand their request clearly before committing. Don't overpromise. If you can't meet their exact needs, offer an alternative and explain why.

This approach is often applied to bosses and business partners, but don't overlook your peers. If you aspire to lead a team as large as the one you're part of, asking your peers what they need becomes vital.

ACTION 3: SELF-EVALUATION

You've figured out what your direct reports and colleagues need from you. Now, it's time to focus on what you need from yourself.

What do you need to provide yourself to be the most productive version of you? You probably have a good grasp of what your direct reports need, and you've hopefully asked your business partners and bosses about their expectations.

With this knowledge, you can now pinpoint what you need to do for yourself to meet these expectations. This might involve adopting disciplines that keep you mentally sharp and physically healthy. It could also mean brushing up on certain skills or learning new ones.

Many leaders, despite their best intentions, overlook this step. They prioritize the needs of others over their own, which is commendable. However, if you don't take care of your own needs, you'll quickly run out of steam to support anyone else. This is where burnout sneaks in, or you start experiencing the law of diminishing returns. So, make sure to take care of yourself too.

STEP 2: PEOPLE PRIORITIES

You're going to follow an 80/20 rule to prioritize your time spent with your people. Namely, 80% of your productivity will come from 20% of your efforts with people. So, you should spend that 20% on the highest priority people to affect the biggest overall impact.

Two different field examples:

Example 1: This is an example of a team that is not optimal. In baseball, this would be like having your 7th best hitter leading off. Your goal is to work towards the smallest deltas between the volume/responsibility rank and the force rank.

VOLUME/RESPONSIBILITY RANK	FORCE RANK	DELTA
1	7	<6>
2	1	<1>
3	10	<7>
4	6	<2>
5	8	<3>
6	3	<3>
7	2	+5
8	5	+3
9	9	Even
10	4	+6

Example 2: This is an example of what you are shooting to achieve. You will notice very small deltas between the volume/responsibility and the force rank. Or when it comes to the field, you may have an anomaly like your #3 force ranked direct report runs your 10th highest volume because it so happens to be an outlier geographically. This person may be both skilled and also required because of its location so it makes sense here.

VOLUME/RESPONSIBILITY RANK	FORCE RANK	DELTA
1	1	Flat
2	3	<1>
3	2	+1
4	4	Flat
5	6	<1>
6	5	+1
7	7	Flat
8	9	<1>
9	8	+1
10	10	Flat

Ok, so you now see your deltas; now what?

ACTION: CREATE YOUR QUARTERLY PEOPLE PLAN

Identify the top three or so people you'll spend most of your time with this quarter—those who are key to boosting business.

Start by tackling the biggest gaps (deltas) between potential

EARN WHILE YOU LEARN

and performance. Once these gaps are minimal, you can focus more on your top talent. As long as there's a mismatch between someone's role and their ranking in your team, you won't reach optimal performance.

Your first task is to create conditions that allow for optimal performance. For instance, if your top two priorities are individuals ranked 7th and 10th but responsible for high-volume tasks, they need your focus. Your third priority might depend on your understanding of the team's dynamics. Also, take note of any significant gaps in other areas, like your top-ranked team members handling lower-volume tasks.

You might wonder how quickly you can minimize these gaps and achieve optimal positioning. Ideally, aim for 1 to 2 quarters. Focus most of your time where the largest gaps exist. This approach will clarify whether someone can rise in the rankings to match their responsibilities. If not, they might need a different role within the company or a new job elsewhere.

How do you decide if demotion is effective? Look at the character practices from this book. If someone is hardworking, open to learning, responsible, and disciplined but still struggles in their current role, they might be more valuable in a different position. However, if they're falling short in these character aspects, it might be time to part ways.

After the first quarter of this plan, you need to take action. Decide if individuals are suitable for their roles and adjust their ranking accordingly. Whether promoting, demoting, or moving on from someone, these decisions will help close the gaps. If you need to replace someone, either promote a high-ranking team member from a lower-volume role or hire externally, aiming to match the new hire's potential with the role's demands. Your external new hires can't be ranked towards the bottom unless they are hired to run one of your lower volume responsibilities. If you are hiring someone to run your 3rd highest volume responsibility they need to be your #2, #3 or #4 ranked leader out of the gate. Think of a free agent in sports: the team signs the person they need to fill a specific role mid-season. Remember, your goal is to make accurate hiring and promotion decisions about 90% of the time, as discussed in the Development pillar.

Closing these gaps is crucial. You can't be an optimal leader, have the best team, regularly achieve top results, or have room for your own development unless these gaps are as narrow as possible. Only then can you truly focus your efforts effectively. This is why 'people' is the first of the 5 P's of performance.

STEP 3: PRODUCT ANALYSIS

The aim here is to figure out which products your company wants you to sell are the most crucial and will give you the best return on your time investment. If you can't tackle everything but manage to focus on these key items, you'll still be on track for success. These products are worth a lot more in terms of revenue. Even if you can cover all your bases, prioritizing the items with the highest return on investment will boost your chances of top-tier performance, possibly even leading to out-standing, gold-medal-level results.

ACTION 1: IDENTIFY SALES DRIVERS

Start by listing the top 5 to 10 products or categories driving sales at the moment. Don't worry about ordering them yet; that comes later, after comparing your performance with the company's overall results. Depending on your role, you might focus on broader categories (like Fleece or Activewear) or specific styles (like Levi 501 or Air Jordan 1). The aim is to identify which products deserve most of your time and effort based on their return on investment (ROI).

Consider whether to focus on current sales volumes or what the company expected to be top sellers. This can be tricky. Your current sales might suggest one priority, while the company's expectations (and inventory investments) might indicate another. If you're not sure which angle to take, ask your boss or colleagues for guidance.

Compare your sales in each category to the company's overall performance. If you're in a unique geographical market, compare your performance to your region instead. For example:

Fleece: You're up 15% from last year, but the company over-all is up 21%. This is a negative delta of 6 points. Your fleece sales are $343,100; if you were in line with the company, you'd have made $363,700, missing out on $20,600.

Denim: You're up 35%, while the company is up 37%. This is a negative delta of 2 points. Your denim sales are $514,500; in line with the company, you'd have made $525,000, missing out on $10,500.

Rank these categories by the volume of sales you're missing out on. In our example, Fleece is a higher priority than Denim because the missed sales are greater, despite Denim being a higher volume category for you.

A side note: Sometimes, a negative delta shouldn't drive your priorities. For instance, if your inventory in a category is much lower than the company average, this might explain the delta, and focusing on it might not be worthwhile (though you should communicate this issue).

Remember, you don't need exact figures. You're looking for insights to guide your priorities, not a precise scientific analysis.

Finally, decide if these priorities are widespread across most of your team or specific to a few areas. For example, if Denim is a problem across eight out of ten stores or districts, it's a broad business issue. But if only three stores are struggling with Denim, focus your efforts there and avoid generalizing the problem.

The worst thing you can do as a leader is to make a general fuss about an issue that only affects a few. This can lead to your team tuning you out, both now and in the future.

ACTION 2: IDENTIFY YOUR FOCUS KPIS

Compile a list of all the key performance indicators (KPIs) and metrics your company currently emphasizes, or those you personally recognize as important. In this step, your aim is to identify which one or two KPIs/metrics should be your focus to get the best return on your efforts. Here are some examples:

- Sales over Traffic

- Average Transaction Value

- Average Unit Retail

- Units Per Transaction

- Conversion Rate

- Gross Margin

- Net Promoter Score

- Credit Card Sign-ups

It's wise to set aside metrics like Sales over Traffic and Average Transaction Value initially. These are broader indicators, often influenced by more specific metrics like Average Unit Retail, Units Per Transaction, and Conversion Rate. Understanding these underlying factors is key to identifying where the gaps are.

While some may argue that Conversion Rate is the most controllable metric in a retail setting, it doesn't automatically mean it's the most crucial metric to focus on. This depends on how your performance stacks up against the company's average.

Similarly, Average Unit Retail and Gross Margin might seem out of your control, but that's not always the case. For example, markdowns or clearance margins can show significant performance differences across locations, depending on how much attention they receive. Moreover, if your store's Average Unit Retail is lower than a comparable store, it could be due to your merchandising strategies for newer or full-price products.

The key in this step is to quantify the impact of these metrics in monetary terms. This helps in prioritizing which KPIs or metrics can most significantly influence your store's financial performance.

SCENARIO

No matter if you're running a store, district, region, or entire company, the same KPIs should apply. The below scenario is one example of a store's numbers; apply this methodology to your own numbers.

- Volume = $430,000

- Total Transactions = 10,000

- Total Units Sold = 25,000

- Average Transaction = $43.00

- Average Unit Retail = $17.20

- Units per Transaction = 2.5

- Conversion 30%

- Traffic 33,335

ASSUMPTIONS

Quick reminder: don't drill down into Sales over Traffic or Average Transaction Value at first. Those metrics are a broader result of the following metrics and don't really stand alone.

- If your Average Unit Retail is $17.20 and the company is $18.00, you have a negative .70 cent delta.

- You need to know how many units you have sold to multiple by this .70 cents you are down in AUR

- Let's say you have sold 25,000 units so far X .70 = $17,500 in sales if you were in line with the company.

- If your Units Per Transaction is 2.5 and the companies is 3.0, you have a negative delta of .5.

- You need to know how many transactions you have had to multiply by the .5.

- 10,000 X .5 = 5,000 additional units would have been sold if in line with the company's 3.0 UPT.

- You would then multiply the $17.20 Average Unit Retail X 5,000 which equals $86,000.

- If your conversion is 30% and the company's is 33%, you have a 3% delta.

- 10,000 transactions X 3% = 300 additional transactions

- 300 transactions X $43.00 Average Transaction = $12,900 in sales if you were in line with the company.

Deciding where to put your time and energy can be tough. But here, UPT stands out as the big opportunity, missing out on $86,000 in sales compared to the rest of the company. Still, you can't just rely on data; your own insights are key. Say you're managing a store or market that usually sees higher average prices than others. This often means your UPT might take a hit. So, in such cases, aiming for a slight improvement in UPT, like a 0.5 increase, might be the way to go. For the scenario mentioned earlier, focusing on improving Conversion, which could add $20,000, might be a smarter move. You need to balance data with your own understanding of the situation. One without the other just doesn't work.

Start with the numbers (the science) and then apply your local knowledge (the art). Relying solely on one without the other won't give you the full picture. Most people lean towards either the science or the art side of things. Recognize which way you lean and either work on developing the opposite skill or collaborate with others in your network who complement your approach.

For metrics like credit card sign-ups, most companies can quantify the value of a credit card customer. You can use this data to figure out your opportunity in that area.

Some KPIs or metrics, like Net Promoter Score, are harder to translate into monetary terms. In these cases, you need to depend more on insights and understanding the intangible benefits.

PRO TIPS FOR REVIEWING METRICS/KPIS

1. Pay attention to differences in Average Unit Retail.

2. Monitor how markdowns are impacting performance.

3. Keep an eye on Gross Margin figures.

4. Look out for variations in Conversion rates.

ACTION 3: THINK OF STORES AS PRODUCTS

SCENARIO

Imagine you're a District Manager overseeing 10 stores.

In this context, think of your 10 stores as products. (For folks at the corporate office, think of your function or team as a "store", and your stores as products in the same way.) The leaders within these stores fall under the 'People' step, but this is a distinct consideration. You might need to prioritize a store even if its leader isn't at the top of your priority list. This scenario becomes more common when you have a well-functioning, optimal team.

Start by listing out the performance of your 10 stores. Look at comparative sales (Comp), sales targets (Plan), and profitability metrics. Hopefully, you have access to this information.

RESPONSI-BILITY	COMP	DELTA TO COMPANY	PLAN	DELTA TO COMPANY	PROFITABILITY
Company	+3%		+1%		
Store 1	+21%	+18	+3%	+2	$258,000
2	+14%	+11	+13%	+12	$1,000
3	+8%	+5	+10%	+9	$210,000
4	+4%	+1	-1%	-2	<$12,600>
5	+1%	-2	-5%	-6	<$21,500>
6	-3%	-6	+0%	-1	$197,000
7	-6%	-9	-7%	-8	$86,700
8	-7%	-10	-13%	-14	<$450>

| 9 | -11% | -14 | -10% | -11 | $178,000 |
| 10 | -23% | -26 | -2% | -3 | $14,500 |

Okay, now that you have the numbers (the science), it's time to apply your insights (the art).

First, look at the profitability column. The most profit is coming from stores 1, 3, 6, and 9. On paper, stores 1 and 3 are doing well in both comparative sales and sales targets. However, stores 6 and 9 are lagging in these areas, possibly because of better rent deals.

Insight-wise, you might realize that stores 1 and 3 are operating at full capacity, but 6 and 9 aren't. By focusing on improving stores 6 and 9, you could potentially increase profits more significantly than by concentrating on other stores.

A common hurdle is that many companies don't provide profitability figures to their leaders. This might be because they're privately owned and want to keep such details confidential, or they may want leaders to focus on metrics that drive stock performance, like comparative sales.

If you don't have access to profitability data, just leave that column out and concentrate on the other metrics.

Returning to our scenario, let's consider stores 4, 5, and 8, which are all losing money. Since the goal is to make a profit, these stores are your starting point. If store 9 is in really bad shape, as indicated by its sales target performance, it might become a priority over one of the loss-making stores. With focused attention for three months, store 9 could potentially contribute more to the bottom line than turning a loss-making store around.

But what if a particular responsibility—in this case, a store—demands more of your time than its leader does? How do you balance your time in this store with the need to spend time with other key leaders? One solution could be to bring those leaders to you while you're working in this store.

PRO TIP FOR REVIEWING COMPARATIVE SALES, PLAN, AND PROFITABILITY

Comp:

1. Don't rely only on a one-year comparison. If a store shows significantly different results compared to others, check a two-year comparative sales analysis. For instance, a store might be up 21% this year, while others are around 1%. However, if last year it was down 20% and others were up 2%, it essentially evens out over two years.

2. Be aware of the environment. Factors like nearby construction affecting traffic or new developments boosting it can influence a store's performance. Use this understanding to set realistic expectations.

Plan:

1. For new stores open for less than a year, the plan percentage is often based on initial projections or rent deal assumptions, which can be inaccurate. This is crucial to remember, especially if the plan is tied to incentives.

2. Companies don't always consider multi-year sales trends when setting future targets. This can lead to unrealistic expectations. For example, if you had a great year last year, this year's target might be set too high, and vice versa.

Profitability:

1. If a store is losing money or earning less than others, examine its rent and expenses. High costs compared to others might be due to a poor rent deal, something the store might not be able to offset. Understanding these

financial nuances can influence how you prioritize different stores.

STEP 4: PRODUCT PRIORITIES

Figure out which product really needs top-notch performance and decide where you can afford to cut back. This will free up the resources needed to focus on what matters most.

As a leader, you represent the organization to your team. If you notice a consistent trend, good or bad, across most of your area, it could be due to a company-wide issue or something in your leadership style.

Take the holiday season, for example, when stress levels skyrocket. Everyone is working harder, feeling more burnt out, and the company's demands are at their highest.

Many leaders try to meet all demands, but a smarter approach is to focus on where you'll get the biggest return on investment. This is where the 80/20 Rule comes in handy.

Your company might hope you can handle everything, but often that's just not possible. That's why it's crucial to prioritize—whether it's the products you're selling, your stores, functions, or key metrics important to the company.

ACTION: PRIORITIZE MOST RESULTS <> LEAST EFFORT

Ask yourself: What work will bring the most results with the least effort? You've just drilled into the data and insights associated with sales drivers, KPIs, and your stores/teams as products. Use this data to determine where you're going to spend the majority of your time with the 80/20 Rule.

Make sure your team focuses on excelling in these areas. Otherwise, you risk ending up with mediocre performance across the board.

Now that you know which talent and products are most and least valuable, you can plan your time more effectively and incorporate this into your overall strategy.

STEP 5: PROCESS

Your aim is to establish routines and disciplines that align with the people and product priorities you've chosen. It's crucial to set up regular check-ins to make sure the processes you're using are leading to the results you want. If they're working, great, keep going. If not, be ready to adapt and make changes. Remember, the goal remains the same, but the way you achieve it might need tweaking.

Think of it like a football game: the defense reacts to your initial plays. Similarly, in a customer-focused business, the environment will respond to your strategies. You might need to adjust your processes, and sometimes even your priorities, to achieve the desired outcome.

ACTION 1: PLAN YOUR SCHEDULE

Plan your schedule so that over 50% of your time is dedicated to your top three people and product priorities.

EXAMPLE QUARTERLY CALENDAR

First, fill in all fixed events to see how much time you have left for your regular work and personal growth. In the example below, only fixed events are shown. You'll notice there are 39 days not allocated for anything specific. I like to keep one "white space" day each month as a buffer for any unexpected changes. This helps me keep my commitments by shifting them to these white space days if needed. With this approach, I'm left with 36 days still open for planning.

	SUN	MON	TUE	WED	THUR	FRI	SAT
Week 1	OFF	ADMIN					OFF
Week 2	OFF	ADMIN			Meet-ing	Meet-ing	OFF
Week 3	OFF	ADMIN				White Space	OFF

Week 4	OFF	PTO	PTO	PTO	PTO	PTO	OFF
Week 5	OFF	ADMIN				AD-MIN	OFF
Week 6	OFF	ADMIN					OFF
Week 7	OFF	ADMIN				White Space	OFF
Week 8	OFF	ADMIN				AD-MIN	OFF
Week 9	OFF	OFF					
Week 10	OFF	ADMIN	Meet-ing	Meet-ing	Meet-ing	Meet-ing	OFF
Week 11	OFF	ADMIN					OFF
Week 12	OFF	ADMIN				White Space	OFF
Week 13	OFF	ADMIN				AD-MIN	OFF

Step 2 in setting up your calendar involves allocating time for your day job, ensuring that your main priorities take up more than 51% of your time. Let's say you decide to dedicate 80% of your time to your day job. That would mean 29 days out of the 36 available (36 Days X 80%), leaving 7 days for personal development (you'll find more about this in the upcoming chapter on Retail University). For the sake of this example, let's assume you have 10 direct reports. Before scheduling your time, it's important to review your priorities.

In the example below, you'll see that I've allocated 5 days each to my top two priorities and 4 days to my third priority. This means that for the remaining direct reports or responsibilities, I can only spare 2 days each in the upcoming quarter.

Twenty-Nine Available days for the Day Job:

DIRECT REPORTS OR RE-SPONSIBILITIES	IF ALL WERE CREATED EQUAL	PRIORITIZED
A	3	5
B	3	5
C	3	4
D	3	3
E	3	2
F	3	2
G	3	2
H	3	2
I	3	2
J	2	2
	29 Days	29 Days

The first step I take is to schedule when I'll meet with each direct report or check on each responsibility, starting with A and moving on to B, and so forth. I do this to spread out my interactions as evenly as possible. By spacing out these visits consistently, I can gauge how much responsibility I can delegate to each direct report. The time between visits, whether it's 3 weeks or 8 weeks, helps me decide how much I can expect them to achieve before our next meeting.

	SUN	MON	TUE	WED	THUR	FRI	SAT
Week 1	OFF	ADMIN	A1	B1	D1	C1	OFF
Week 2	OFF	ADMIN	E1	F1	Meeting	Meeting	OFF
Week 3	OFF	ADMIN	G1	A2	B2	White Space	OFF
Week 4	OFF	PTO	PTO	PTO	PTO	PTO	OFF
Week 5	OFF	ADMIN	C2	D2		ADMIN	OFF
Week 6	OFF	ADMIN	H1		A3	B3	OFF
Week 7	OFF	ADMIN	I1	J1	D3	White Space	OFF
Week 8	OFF	ADMIN	G2		C3	ADMIN	OFF
Week 9	OFF	OFF	A4	E2	B4		J2
Week 10	OFF	ADMIN	Meeting	Meeting	Meeting	Meeting	OFF
Week 11	OFF	ADMIN		F2		C4	OFF

Week 12	OFF	ADMIN	D4		H2	White Space	OFF
Week 13	OFF	ADMIN	I2	B5	A5	AD-MIN	OFF

Step 3 in creating your schedule is to decide how you'll use the remaining days, which are not yet allocated. These days should focus on your personal development. We'll go into more detail about this in the upcoming Retail University example. For now, just keep in mind that these are the empty spaces in your schedule.

ACTION 2: PLAY CHESS

When managing people, think like a chess master, not a checkers player.

You might wonder how to keep everything else on track if you're spending most of your time (over 50%) with just three key people. It's a valid concern.

The solution lies in focusing on the one or two areas you identified for each person to improve at the start of this process. Many of these areas can be addressed over the phone, just as effectively as in person. You can have productive discussions while driving between locations or during a quick snack break in the office. Another strategy is to have other team members join you when you're working with your top three priorities.

Additionally, make good use of your top performers. They

set the standard for the rest of the team. Even if they haven't reached their peak yet, they're currently your best, and their actions should motivate others. Look for opportunities to amplify their influence.

You'll be able to focus more on developing these top performers once your situation is more optimal, with minimal gaps, and when you can afford to spend more time with them. Until then, use their skills and influence wisely.

ACHIEVING MASTERY

When you've mastered the 5Ps, and having done the work of this chapter day in and day out to develop yourself and your team, you've earned the right to start focusing on yourself.

Don't feel selfish about this. Most people I know in retail feel selfish if they focus on themselves at all; they're so used to giving all their energy to other people and efforts. But this is where you're going to really level up by bringing some of that focus back to you.

What we just did was create a development funnel. We started at the broadest level and narrowed it down until your efforts are prioritized on the most important few.

If you've mastered what's in this chapter, it's time for YOU to level up. Your team needs you to level up. It's like my earlier story—I'd run out of things to offer the team, so I needed to level up in order to continue to offer them great leadership.

Most people won't put in the effort to deliver consistent results—about 8 out of 10, to be precise. It's too much work for them. But I want you to be among the 1 or 2 who do put in the effort.

The 5 P's is your key to success at work and, over time, to giving more attention to your personal development and life.

The concept of the 5 P's—performance driven by People and Product Prioritized, supported by Processes, leading to Productivity—is meant to integrate smoothly into your everyday language. It's about practical application, not just a theory. These principles are designed to keep you at the top of your game, consistently aiming for the gold, silver, or bronze. The idea is that by always being in the mix, you're more likely to win big over time.

This approach is a powerful tool for peak performance, whether you're working solo or leading a team. It emphasizes putting people first, closely followed by the product.

Recognizing that not everything is equally important highlights the job's complexity, underlining the importance of routines to maintain focus and achieve long-term success.

CHAPTER TEN

RETAIL UNIVERSITY

I made the decision when I was 17 years old not to go to college.

I made this decision because I hated school at the time, and preferred working. I have been working since I was twelve years old. The lure of being able to afford the next pair of Nike Air Jordans was too much for me. At the time I just couldn't see myself voluntarily going to school for another 4 years, and then getting a "real job". I also didn't have the money, and thankfully didn't really understand the loan process all that well.

I needed more immediate gratification (this may just be my ADHD, but I've also noticed the need for instant gratification as a trait in tons of people who have chosen retail). I was already working fulltime as a key holder for a company called Chess King in White Plains, New York. As I mentioned in my introduction, I already understood what the path to becoming a Vice President and the corner office was, so, I asked myself, can I grow into the next level which is district manager role in the same amount of time it would take me to graduate college?

And the answer was yes. It was very clear to me.

I decided I was going to put together my own education. My own 3 to 5 year plan. I was going to figure out how to recreate the education process to my advantage and do it in a way that I could enjoy. I always loved learning; I just didn't like being told what I had to learn.

The first step in this process was to begin with the end in mind. I had not yet read Stephen Covey's 7 Habits book yet, but I had always thought this way. I loved problem solving, especially because you were told what the problem was. Your job was to figure that shit out and the dopamine rushes my non-diagnosed ADHD brain (more on this in a later book) got from the anticipation of solving a problem was exhilarating.

If I wanted to be a District Manager in the same time it took to graduate college, I needed to clearly understand what one looked like. I was privileged enough to be able to be around some really good district managers at the time I was with Chess King.

I then started to ask myself questions:

1. What was I already good at that I could leverage?

2. What wasn't I good at, that I would have to learn?

3. What was I terrified of, that I would have to overcome?

Once I answered these 3 questions, I was able to build out a loose plan and start doing the work.

A couple examples of my answers:

I was a salesman and a high energy communicator. I had a lot of confidence, many would say at the time it was arrogance, but I really don't care what anybody thought about me. I was able to withstand mistake after mistake, and not feel bad about myself.

I was a terrible operator, had low attention spans, and didn't like taking direction from anyone.

I was terrified of recruiting and although I wasn't terrified of performance managing an under performer, I would prefer to uplift folks.

This was where I started. And this plan took me where I wanted to go. In this chapter, we're going to put pen to paper and design your own plan.

RETAIL UNIVERSITY

Now that we're on track with our day jobs and consistently achieving success, it's time to focus on our own growth. Often in retail, regardless of the role, most people spend nearly all their time thinking about their team and not enough about themselves.

Why is this an issue? If you're not growing, you can't offer much to your team as situations and needs evolve. By investing in your own development, you're not just setting yourself up for advancement, but you're also creating opportunities for everyone around you.

What if you're not looking to climb the ladder and are happy where you are? Should you still focus on personal growth? Absolutely. To maintain your position, or even consider moving up, you need to keep pace with industry changes and grow in your role.

Let's break down the levels of personal development:

Level 1 is about building your independence. If you're just starting out or feeling stuck, this level helps you become more self-reliant. It focuses on outworking and outlearning others, with an introduction to being the example, being accountable, and being disciplined.

Level 2 is about becoming best in class independently. You should be gaining confidence and outperforming most. This level reinforces being the example, being accountable, and being disciplined.

Level 3 shifts the focus from 'you' to 'we'. It's about interdependence and leading others. You'll develop skills in team development and communication, with a nod to influence. This level is for those who are successful and starting to gain followers.

Level 4 takes interdependence to the best in class level. With a larger following and more impact on the company's success, this level emphasizes influence. Your skills in development, communication, and influence are crucial for engaging with your boss, their boss, and your team.

How do you know what level you're currently at?

1. Level 1: If you're not regularly on the podium, you're here.

2. Level 2: Consistent success due to your efforts puts you here.

3. Level 3: Consistent success with followers means you're here.

4. Level 4: If you're successful, have followers moving up but feel stuck yourself, you're here.

5. Graduated: Consistent success, followers advancing, and you're still climbing. You've mastered all levels.

Your goals and the time you invest in personal development shape your progress. Changing jobs or companies can reset your progress as you demonstrate your capabilities to new leaders or teams. But, with the skills you've mastered, adapting to new environments can be efficient and smooth, as long as you keep your ego in check and focus on learning quickly in new roles.

Typically, each level of advancement takes 3 to 5 years, whether that means a new role or more responsibilities. Faster progress indicates mastery of these practices, while slower progress might be due to less focus on personal development, either by choice or circumstance.

LEVEL 1: INDEPENDENT 1.0

ATTENDEES

You are either new in your role or not making it to the podium often in your day job.

OVERVIEW

This level focuses on two key practices that are crucial for your success and career growth. It doesn't matter what role or level you're currently in—whether you're a new sales associate or further up the career ladder. What's important is your willingness to roll up your sleeves, your curiosity, and your eagerness to learn. You'll need to let go of the past and not worry about the future to fully engage with this course. By the end, you should be outperforming not just your past self but also most, if not all, of your peers. The skills you develop here will not only help you in future courses but will also be valuable in your life for many years to come.

LEARNING OBJECTIVES

Through Outworking and Outlearning, you will be able to:

1. Be more determined, resilient, attentive, perseverant and patient.

2. Exhibit greater integrity.

3. Exhibit greater Self control

4. Feel a greater sense of fulfillment

5. Improve problem solving skills

6. Improve your critical thinking and presentation skills

MATERIALS

Outlook:

Keep a calendar for both your work and personal life. This will help you stay organized and maintain discipline.

Social Media:

As a retailer or leader, one of the best ways to learn is by teaching. Share your experiences on social media. This encourages engagement and creates a community where everyone can learn from each other. Also, social media can often be one of the best places to learn. Take a look at what other people are doing and see what insights you can learn from them.

Audible or Kindle:

To absorb as much knowledge as possible, consider listening to books or podcasts. You can do this while running, at the gym, or during your commute.

Recommended Reading:

1. *7 Habits of Highly Effective People* by Stephen R. Covey

2. *212: The Extra Degree* by Sam Parker and Mac Anderson

3. *Stop Doing That Sh*t: End Self-Sabotage and Demand Your Life Back* by Gary John Bishop

4. *Unfu*k Yourself: Get Out of Your Head and into Your Life* by Gary John Bishop

5. *The Subtle Art of Not Giving a F*ck* by Mark Manson

6. *Good to Great: Why Some Companies Make the Leap and Others Don't* by Jim Collins

7. *Sam Walton: Made in America* by Sam Walton and John Huey

8. *Nuts! Southwest Airlines' Crazy Recipe for Business and Personal Success* by Kevin Freiberg and Jackie Freiberg

9. *Coach Wooden's Pyramid of Success* by John Wooden and Jay Carty

10. *Leaders Eat Last: Why Some Teams Pull Together and Others Don't* by Simon Sinek

11. *Find Your Why: A Practical Guide for Discovering Purpose for You and Your Team* by Simon Sinek

12. *The 5 AM Club: Own Your Morning, Elevate Your Life* by Robin Sharma

13. *If I Knew Then What I Know Now* by Richard Edler

14. *25 Management Lessons from the Customer's Side of the Counter* by James H. Donnelly Jr.

STRUCTURE

This course, like all others in this series, is self-directed, and your progress depends on your commitment and results. Only you can judge whether you've given it your all and if you're drained at the end of each day. Your frequent successes, both personally and professionally, will be a clear indicator of your progress.

You'll need to balance three key areas of your life:

1. Life Outside of Work: This includes quality time with family and friends or just for yourself. Activities could range from golfing, spa visits, attending sports events with your kids, watching TV, or having date nights.

2. Work (Your Day Job): This is what pays the bills.

3. Your Coursework (Retail University): This focuses on your personal development.

At this point, you're likely dedicating a significant portion of your time to your day job, say about 56 hours a week, or roughly a third of your time. Assuming you sleep 8 hours a night, that's another third of your time gone. This leaves you with another 56 hours to split between your personal life and your coursework.

A typical university student might spend 12 to 16 hours per week in class. Let's say you aim for 10 to 14 hours per week on your coursework, which breaks down to about 1.5 to 2 hours per day.

That leaves you with about 30 to 34 hours for activities outside of work. For many, this might not seem like enough time. I personally have found ways to borrow some time from my sleep, largely due to the exercise routine I use to kickstart my days.

Note: As you ascend from Level 1–Level 4, the split of time you'll be spending on your day job versus your own development and your personal life will start to shift in weight. Early on, you'll be weighted toward your day job. As you level up, you'll start to open up more time for your home life and personal development.

CIRCUMSTANCES

Everyone starts Retail University from different places in life, impacting which Level you start on. You might have a lot of free time outside work, or you could be juggling a large family and extra responsibilities that need your time and attention.

The length of time you'll need for this course varies. It might take you 6 months, or it could take 2 years, and that's perfectly fine. It all depends on your personal schedule and how much time you can dedicate to the course. For instance, if you can spend 20 hours a week on it, you'll likely progress faster than someone who can only spare 3 to 4 hours weekly. Also, you might already have a head start in some areas covered by the course, which can speed up your completion.

The first two pillars of this book are designed to help you pinpoint where to focus your time and provide insights on how you can improve.

Before diving into any course, I suggest you do a quick self-assessment. On a scale of 1 to 10, how would you rate yourself in terms of outworking and outlearning? Picture a 10 as being completely drained at the end of the day, and a 1 as being idle and unproductive. You'll likely find yourself somewhere in between. Think about what's holding you back from scoring a 10, and consider how you can incorporate those improvements into your schedule.

SCHEDULE

To effectively tackle this course, divide it into calendar quarters. Start by adding any fixed personal events you have scheduled, like vacations, days off, doctor's appointments, etc. For work, mark down fixed events such as administrative or office days, meetings, or any other commitments that require your presence and can't be rescheduled. These are your essentials.

Next, look at your electives—where do you want to focus your efforts based on your 5 P's of performance?

With a 13-week schedule that balances work and life, how will you find time for your course activities? When will you read or listen to a book or podcast that enhances your skills in outworking or outlearning? Fit these into your existing schedule. Consider times when you're commuting, in a hotel, or have free evenings or mornings. Match your course work with your day job activities that align with practicing outworking and outlearning. Be strategic and thoughtful with your planning. Consider potential hurdles and leave some white space in your calendar for flexibility. This way, if something unexpected comes up, you can shift it into your free time later in the quarter.

Referring back to the Process section from the previous chapter on the 5 P's of performance, decide how you'll use the 7 development days you've set aside (remember, this is 20% of your available time after accounting for fixed events and work commitments). Input these plans into your schedule. If you're at a stage where you're not regularly achieving top results, and you're learning this level, your team might be in the same boat. A great approach is to involve them in your learning journey by organizing workshops or group learning sessions.

	SUN	MON	TUE	WED	THUR	FRI	SAT
Week 1	OFF	ADMIN	A1	B1	D1	C1	OFF
Week 2	OFF	ADMIN	E1	F1	Meeting	Meeting	OFF
Week 3	OFF	ADMIN	G1	A2	B2	White Space	OFF
Week 4	OFF	PTO	PTO	PTO	PTO	PTO	OFF
Week 5	OFF	ADMIN	C2	D2	Outwork workshop 1.0	AD-MIN	OFF
Week 6	OFF	ADMIN	H1	Learning Agility Workshop	A3	B3	OFF
Week 7	OFF	ADMIN	I1	J1	D3	White Space	OFF
Week 8	OFF	ADMIN	G2	Growth Mindset Workshop	C3	AD-MIN	OFF
Week 9	OFF	OFF	A4	E2	B4	Coachability workshop	J2
Week 10	OFF	ADMIN	Meeting	Meeting	Meeting	Meeting	OFF
Week 11	OFF	ADMIN	Outwork Workshop 2.0	F2	Inspiration Trip	C4	OFF

Week 12	OFF	ADMIN	D4	Fixed Mindset Work-shop	H2	White Space	OFF
Week 13	OFF	ADMIN	I2	B5	A5	AD-MIN	OFF

I recommend adding recurring events to your Outlook calendar as well. Here are some examples:

- Daily, 7 am 8 am: Run 5 miles while listening to a specific book or podcast.

- 8:30 am 9:15 am: Listen to a book or podcast during my morning commute.

- 6 pm 6:45 pm: Listen to a book or podcast on my way home.

If I'm traveling or know there are days when I can't stick to these routines, I won't set them as recurring. Instead, I'll schedule them for specific days when I'm able to follow through.

EXPECTATIONS

To succeed in this course, you need to be fully committed to doing the work. If you're only somewhat interested, you'll likely give up or lose momentum at the first hurdle.

Here's an example to illustrate the point:

Scenario 1: You're interested in running. One morning, you wake up to freezing temperatures and rain. You tell yourself, "I'll run tomorrow," and you don't run.

Scenario 2: You're committed to running. Despite waking up to freezing, rainy weather, you either brave the elements in your shorts or find a treadmill indoors. Regardless, you make sure you run.

I expect that by the end of each day, you'll be tired but also feel a strong sense of achievement.

GRADING PHILOSOPHY

You'll know you've completed this course when you're regularly making it to the podium. That means consistently ranking 1st, 2nd, or 3rd in most of your organization's key metrics. Your 'organization' could be a single store, a group of stores, a specific function, or several functions.

Expect to be both physically and mentally tired at the end of each day. This fatigue comes from the effort you're putting in—both the physical work and the amount of information you're absorbing. If you find you still have energy to spare when you go to bed, it's a sign you can push yourself a bit more.

FIT TEST

On a scale of 1 to 10, how would you rate yourself in the following areas?

1. How hard are you working?

2. How open are you to learning new things?

3. How often do you put into practice what you've learned?

4. How coachable are you?

If you're scoring between 8 and 10 in all these areas, you should be achieving top results more often than not. If you're not, it might be time to reevaluate your self-assessment.

Think about what changes you need to make to confidently rate yourself between 8 and 10 in each category.

LEVEL 2: INDEPENDENT 2.0

For Materials, Structure, Circumstances, Schedule, and Expectations, see Level 1.

ATTENDEES

This level is for those who are either new in their roles or find themselves with few followers, meaning they often have to do most of the work to achieve success.

OVERVIEW

This level focuses on being the example, being accountable, and being disciplined. You'll learn to motivate others through your actions, take full control of your outcomes, and maintain your path to success and happiness, even when it's tough. To succeed here, you must apply the practices from Level 1. Without hard work and a willingness to learn, you can't set an example or sustain the energy needed for accountability and discipline. These practices, combined with those from Level 1, pave the way to move from being independent to interdependent, similar to transitioning from a teenager to an adult. By the end of this course, you should be able to work independently, make mistakes without constant supervision, and be self-sufficient.

LEARNING OBJECTIVES

1. By being exemplary, accountable, and disciplined, you'll be able to:

2. Manage your behavior effectively

3. Stay more focused and attentive

4. Enhance your reputation

5. Build trust and credibility, boosting team engagement and commitment

6. Gain a stronger sense of control, happiness, and fulfillment

7. Reduce anxiety and stress

8. Grow your influence

9. Improve productivity and time management

10. Make better decisions

11. Achieve better overall performance

RECOMMENDED READING

1. *The Tao of Personal Leadership* by Lao Tzu and Diane

Dreher

2. *The 4 Disciplines of Execution* by Sean Covey, Chris McChesney, and Jim Huling

3. *The 5 Dysfunctions of a Team* by Patrick Lencioni

4. *Willpower Doesn't Work* by Ben Hardy

5. *Atomic Habits* by James Clear

6. *The Compound Effect* by Darren Hardy

7. *Grit* by Angela Duckworth

8. *21 Irrefutable Laws of Leadership* by John Maxwell

9. *Developing the Leader within You* by John Maxwell

10. *Strengths Based Leadership* by Tom Rath & Barry Conchie

11. *It Takes What It Takes* by Trevor Moawad

12. *Time Tactics of Very Successful People* by B. Eugene

Griessman

13. *The 10 Natural Laws of Successful Time and Life Management* by Hyrum W. Smith

14. *The Power of Now* by Eckhart Tolle

15. *Great by Choice* by Jim Collins and Morten T. Hansen

GRADING PHILOSOPHY

You'll know you've completed this course when you've gained more followers while consistently achieving top results. More people in your workplace should view you as a role model, exemplifying the behaviors they want to emulate. Your followers may not be getting promoted yet—that's for the next level.

You should feel more in control of your decisions and actions, with your work environment having less impact on how you operate. Instead of feeling exhausted, you should end each day feeling refreshed and energized.

Now, you're ready to share your knowledge and experiences with others, helping them climb the ladder too.

FIT TEST

Rate yourself on a scale of 1 to 10 for the following:

1. How well are you setting an example for others?

2. Are you acknowledging (mind) and embracing (heart) your reality?

3. Are you showing accountable behaviors (embracing

4. reality, finding solutions, and making things happen)?

5. How effectively are you managing your time?

6. Are you maintaining the best mindset?

7. Are you making the decisions that allow you to be fully alert and available during your workday (lifestyle)

8. Are you adding the word "yet" to any sentence that includes "I can't"?

If you're scoring between 8 and 10 in all these areas, you're likely achieving top results frequently and have a strong following.

If you're not meeting these benchmarks, take a moment to reassess. Consider what changes you need to make to confidently rate yourself between 8 and 10 in each category.

LEVEL 3: INTERDEPENDENT 1.0

For Materials, Structure, Circumstances, Schedule, and Expectations, see Level 1.

ATTENDEES

You are making it to the podium more often than not, and you have a good amount of followers. However you find that your followers are not progressing at the rate you would like—yet!

OVERVIEW

At this stage, the impact of others on your success becomes more significant. You'll move from focusing on yourself (YOU) to working with others (WE). This level teaches you how to develop yourself further, creating more opportunities to help others grow. You'll learn effective communication, keeping the other person's understanding in mind. Towards the end of this course, we'll also start exploring the concept of influence. To take on this level, you should have completed Level 1 and 2 successfully. If you're not consistently achieving top results, you might not be ready for the challenges this level presents. If you're not highly accountable and disciplined, you may find this course particularly tough.

This level is less about physical effort and more about mental strategy. Your mindset needs to align with the course objectives. By the end, you should have gained more followers, both directly and indirectly, and they should be achieving their own successes and moving up. You'll find yourself spending more time planning your communication to ensure it's effective and meets the needs of your audience.

LEARNING OBJECTIVES

Through Development and Communication, you will be able to:

1. Have a better work/life integration

2. Better direction

3. Increased morale, motivation, confidence, productivity and knowledge for yourself and everyone in your

hemisphere.

4. Improve career prospects

5. Increased Skill sets

6. Improved self-control

7. Feel momentum in your life and in the life of those in your hemisphere

8. Increased self-awareness and self-confidence

9. Better relationships

10. Handle conflict better

11. Have increased empathy for yourself and others

12. Build greater trust in those in your hemisphere

RECOMMENDED READING

1. *How to Win Friends & Influence People* by Dale Carnegie

2. *Emotional Intelligence* by Daniel Goleman

3. *Emotional Intelligence 2.0* by Travis Bradberry & Jean Greaves

4. *Ego is the Enemy* by Ryan Holiday

5. *The Magic of Thinking Big* by David J. Schwartz

6. *Personality isn't Permanent* by Ben Hardy

7. *The Platinum Rule* by Michael J. O'Connor and Tony J. Alessandra

8. *The Personality Compass* by Diane Turner and Thelma Greco

9. *Radical Candor* by Kim Scott

10. *The Obstacle is the Way* by Ryan Holiday

11. *Multipliers* by Liz Wiseman

12. *The 80/20 Individual* by Richard Koch

13. *The 80/20 Principle* by Richard Koch

14. *Get Out of Your Own Way* by Mark Goulston and Phillip Goldberg

15. *Dare to Lead* by Brené Brown

16. *The 17 Indisputable Laws of Teamwork* by John C. Maxwell

17. *Messages: The Communication Skills Book* by McKay, Davis & Fanning

18. *A Whole New Mind* by Daniel Pink

19. *The Definitive Book of Body Language* by Allan and Barbara Pease

20. *Thinking For a Change: 11 Ways Highly Successful People Approach Life and Work* by John C Maxwell

21. *What to Say to Get What You Want* by Sam Deep and Lyle Sussman

22. *Crucial Conversations: Tools For Talking When Stakes Are*

High by Patterson, Greeny, McMillan and Switzler

23. *A Whole New Mind: Why Right Brainers Will Rule the Future* by Daniel Pink

STRUCTURE

At this point in your journey, you can start shifting more time towards your personal development. This change is possible because you've improved at developing others and your communication skills are boosting your productivity, giving you more free time.

Let's say, for example, you can now handle your day job in 44 hours instead of the 56 hours it took during the first two courses. This frees up 12 hours for other activities.

You might choose to dedicate all these 12 hours to your own development, or to your personal life, or split them between both.

In the earlier courses, you may have spent 10 to 14 hours on coursework or personal development. But now, you're investing 16 to 20 hours in these areas. Your time spent on self-improvement has increased from around 7% to 11 or 12%. It's at this stage that you might see a significant acceleration in your career progression.

GRADING PHILOSOPHY

You'll know you've completed this course when the people you're responsible for, those you work alongside, and those you work for start achieving top results more often. You should also start seeing some of these individuals getting promoted. The focus shifts from your own success to their success.

At the end of each day, you're likely to feel more mentally than physically tired. You'll spend more time planning your actions and words than actually executing them. You should be proactive about 98% of the time, rather than reactive.

This level might bring you the best work-life balance you've experienced in years.

FIT TEST

On a scale of 1 to 10, how would you rate the following?

1. Are you flipping the pyramid and working for your team?

2. Are you conducting open book tests by being clear with what the answers to the test are?

3. Are you seeing it and saying it within 24 hours?

4. Are you requiring those you communicate with to reflect back their understanding of what you have said and are you doing the same for your boss and their boss?

5. Are you looking to catch people doing things right, first?

If you're scoring between 8 and 10, you're likely achieving top results frequently and have a significant number of followers who are progressing in their careers.

If you're not meeting these benchmarks, it's time to reassess. Think about what changes you need to make to confidently rate yourself between 8 and 10 in each area.

LEVEL 4: INTERDEPENDENT 2.0

For Materials, Structure, Circumstances, Schedule, and Expectations, see Level 1.

ATTENDEES

This course is for those who consistently achieve top results, have a solid following, and see their followers advancing, but find their own personal growth has plateaued.

OVERVIEW

This course will build on development and communication, but its main focus is on influence—both internally and externally. You'll transition from being interdependent to excelling in interdependence. You'll learn to intentionally use your actions and words to guide others, whether they're your colleagues, subordinates, or superiors. To enroll, you should have completed Level 1, 2, and 3. You'll need to be consistently successful, skilled in developing others, and proficient in communication, particularly from the receiver's point of view. Effective planning of conversations is also crucial. By the end of this course, you should master the art of strategic influence, making and anticipating moves like a chess master.

LEARNING OBJECTIVES

With improved influencing skills, you'll be able to:

1. Achieve long-term goals more easily

2. Lead teams or organizations more effectively

3. Interact with influential groups more frequently

4. Boost your self-confidence and self-esteem

5. Communicate more effectively

6. Gain more from your conversations

7. Negotiate better for yourself and others

8. Resolve conflicts quickly or prevent them from occurring

9. Persuade others of your viewpoints

10. Be more strategic in your approach

RECOMMENDED READING

1. *Walking Through Anger* by Christian Conte (Communication and Influence)

2. *Driven* by Douglas Brackmann and Randy Kelley (if you have ADHD or want to have a greater respect for this behavior)

3. *Leadership and Self-Deception* by The Arbinger Institute (Supports new transitions)

4. *Talk Like Ted* by Carmine Gallo

5. *Stillness is the Key* by Ryan Holiday

6. *Daring Greatly* by Brené Brown

7. *The Effective Executive* by Peter Drucker

8. *The Essential Drucker* by Peter Drucker

9. *Influencer* by Patterson, Greeny, Maxfield, McMillian and Switzler

10. *Built to Last* by Jim Collins and Jerry Porras

11. *Nuts: Southwest Airlines Crazy Recipe for Business and Personal Success* by Kevin Freiberg and Jackie Freiberg

STRUCTURE

Like all the courses in this series, this one is self-paced, and completion depends on the results achieved by those around you in your work environment.

Now, the success of your leaders and peers plays a significant role in your own success. In Level 3, you focused a lot on development and communication to help others grow and advance. To reach that next level for yourself, you'll need to be proactive and skilled at influencing people at all levels— whether they're your peers, subordinates, or superiors.

You'll find yourself in a position where you can greatly impact the careers and businesses of your leaders and peers, thanks to the time and effort you're able to invest in them.

At this point in your journey, you're shifting more time towards developing your influence skills and using them to support the leaders and bosses around you.

For example, let's say you've managed to streamline your day job tasks, completing them in 40 hours instead of 44, as in Level 3. This frees up an additional 4 hours. Ideally, at this stage, you should use this extra time to invest in the success of your leaders and peers.

Previously, in the third level, you might have dedicated 16 to 20 hours to coursework or personal development. Now, you're increasing that time to 20 to 24 hours.

GRADING PHILOSOPHY

You'll know you've completed this course when you continue to advance in your career, alongside the people you're responsible for, those you work with, and those you work for. Naturally, you should still be consistently achieving top results.

At this stage, you should feel less tired than you have in a long time. You'll likely spend more time helping your boss and their superiors improve their performance than focusing on anyone else.

FIT TEST

On a scale of 1-10, how would you rate the following?

1. Are you aware of your personality traits and triggers when stressed?

2. Are you acting on your selfish tendencies for good?

3. Are you avoiding taking yourself too seriously?

4. Are you being intentional with your emotions?

5. Are you meeting your boss and their boss 51% of the way?

If you are an 8-10 in all of these, you should be on the podium more often than you are not, have a great amount of followers who are getting promoted, and you are still ascending.

If you are not these things, reassess your self assessment.

> Ask yourself what you need to begin doing differently in order to confidently say you are between 8 and 10.

NEVER STOP LEVELING UP

Graduating from college or university gives you a diploma to hang on your wall, along with, hopefully, a wealth of knowledge. But if you've come up through the school of hard knocks or Retail University, you might not have a diploma, but you've got the scars and stories that have shaped your character and laid the groundwork for your success, not to mention just as much valuable knowledge.

If you've got a college degree, make sure you match the hustle of those who didn't go to college during your years of study. This means outworking, outlearning, setting an example, and being disciplined and accountable. It's how you build confidence in yourself and earn the trust of others.

For those who didn't attend college, it's crucial to learn how to develop, communicate, influence, and plan—skills that your college-educated peers might have touched on academically while you focused on honing your practical abilities. This is your chance to prove to yourself and others that you've got both the potential and the performance to back it up.

Remember, within 3 to 5 years, you can acquire the

knowledge needed to excel in your role. This journey involves evolving from being dependent to independent, and eventually to being interdependent. And with each new role, responsibility, or boss, it's important to apply this growth cycle all over again.

PILLAR THREE WRAP-UP

Earning while learning is a game-changer when it comes to leading others. To be a good leader, you've got to keep growing and trying new things yourself. This isn't about being selfish; actually, it's the opposite. Making time to learn and improve means you'll have more to share with your team.

If you're learning something new, don't just keep it in your head. Try it out, make mistakes, and learn from them. That's how you really grow. If you want to lead and inspire others, you've got to keep pushing yourself to learn and do more. It's about getting out there, trying new things, and not being afraid to fail because that's how you get better. And when you get better, you help everyone around you get better, too.

Ask yourself these four questions:

1. Am I making it to the podium more often than not?

2. Do I find myself with a good amount of followers?

3. Are my followers getting promoted and or ascending?

4. Am I still getting promoted or ascending?

If you answered NO to any of the above instead of YES, you have more work to do.

Leadership in retail, or really any field, benefits from a blend of formal education and real-world experience. Having only one can put you at a disadvantage compared to those who balance both. Education isn't limited to the classroom, and hard work isn't just for those without a degree. The trick is to identify and fill in whatever gaps you might have, depending on your path.

CONCLUSION

IT'S UP TO YOU

In every formal classroom I've been in over the last 30 years, there's always been a focus on understanding other people. But I think that's backwards. You have to understand yourself first, and only then can you understand others.

Early in my career, when I first took a personality test, I was upset with the results. I was more responsive than assertive, which wasn't what I expected. I thought I would never be like my idol, Michael Jordan, because I cared more about what people thought. But when I started to understand the strengths that came with my responsiveness, I began to appreciate and leverage it.

To me, the most important thing is first understanding how you tick and respecting it. We all have personalities, we're all selfish, and we all have egos. Recognizing these aspects in ourselves allows us to acknowledge and accept them in others.

This book is about YOU and what you can control to

influence your career and the careers of others. You should focus on yourself first before leading others. If you don't, you're not just holding yourself back—you're also hindering others. This could prevent them from earning more and progressing in their careers.

At first glance, this book might seem theoretical, but it's entirely based on practical application. I have personally used this model to achieve every role in my career. Reflecting back, I can clearly see where I was misfiring within this model each time I felt stuck.

This isn't just about manifesting; it's about visualizing your goals so you can write them down and start working backwards from them, tracking milestones along the way. All of this is about understanding how to be the best version of yourself both at work and at home. It's about being engaged and present wherever you are, whether it's with your family or at your job.

THREE TO FIVE YEAR GOALS

You can accomplish anything in three to five years if you treat your role like a college education. It usually takes no more than 3 to 5 years to become an expert in anything, provided you clearly define what being an expert entails and work backwards, creating necessary sprints or milestones for development.

Why 3 to 5 years? Because mastering any role is like getting an education. It requires you to start as an underclassman, where you develop the fundamentals. Then, as an upperclassman, you leverage these basics to dive into the more complex aspects of the role.

You can become an expert closer to the 3 or 4-year mark if you stay focused every day of the year. This means not taking a 'semester' off (stopping paying attention and learning), not changing your 'major' (company), or making similar shifts.

This is why you should always set a goal with two different time frames in mind. Five years is your realistic timeframe, and three years is your ambitious one. From my experience, when you do this, you'll often find yourself achieving your goals somewhere in between these two timeframes.

So many companies and leaders talk about goals as if they are behaviors. The actual goal often gets lost in a series of run-on sentences. They do this because they believe there is only one way to achieve the goal: their way. So, they outline the behaviors they think are necessary instead of simply stating the goal and allowing those responsible for achieving it to decide on the best behaviors.

People need to know the metric or end result they are tasked with and have the freedom to design the way to achieve it. A few examples of goals might be:

1. Deliver a +5% sales comp in Quarter 1.

2. Improve your NPS by 10% by the end of Quarter 2.

3. Develop your succession plan or have an external succession by the end of Quarter 3.

For people to be emotionally, not just rationally, connected to the work, they need to be part of creating it. The fact that people are significantly more productive when emotionally connected to their work should be enough reason to approach goal-setting this way.

Companies and leaders need to set aside their ego and accept that there are multiple ways to achieve a goal. It's not about being right; it's about getting it right. Realizing that someone else might find another way to achieve something you thought had only one solution doesn't mean you were wrong; it just means they were also right.

Now, be smarter than the companies and leaders we've talked about when creating your goals. Take control of your career. Consider what your bosses want, but also include your own goals. For example:

1. Improve my business acumen by the end of Quarter 1.

2. Develop two leaders to succeed me by the end of Quarter 2.

3. Lose 15lbs by the end of Quarter 3.

4. Deliver a +13% comp for the year.

You should be able to quickly state your goals: "I aim to improve my business acumen, develop two potential successors, lose 15lbs, and deliver a 13% comp."

Only after clarifying what you want to achieve should you start planning how to do it. The goal remains constant, but the methods to achieve it can change. You might list behaviors under each goal, but since they are not the goal itself, you can modify, adapt, or completely change them. This means you must constantly evaluate the behaviors you've chosen.

When behaviors are tied into goal statements, if things aren't going as planned, you might end up scrapping the goal instead of adjusting the associated behaviors.

A SERIES OF SPRINTS

I said before that your career is a series of sprints, not a marathon. Success is about achieving a series of milestones that collectively lead to a significant achievement. It's about the effort you put into each inning of the game or every quarter. Your career will go through transformation over time, not just change—change is smaller incremental differences made milestone to milestone, whereas transformation is the entire journey made up of many changes over time.

There's a principle called the Compound Effect, which suggests that small, consistent efforts lead to significant results over time. It's not about one big leap but about many small steps that accumulate and compound into something much greater.

I've also realized that satisfaction is fleeting; you'll always crave more. So when you achieve a goal, celebrate it, but don't act as if it's the only thing you've ever achieved. Barry Sanders, the famous football player, didn't make a huge celebration on each touchdown. He understood that each success was part of a larger journey. Similarly, Kobe Bryant, despite a poor performance one year leading to a title loss, went on to win five championships. Their attitudes towards both success and failure offer valuable lessons on maintaining perspective and focusing on the long-term journey rather than getting lost in the immediate outcomes.

If you don't meet a goal, don't be too hard on yourself. Life offers thousands more opportunities for both success and failure.

A DAY WELL LIVED

Let's end where we started. Walk with me.

Let's get up and go together. Let's not hit the snooze button any longer. Let's put two feet on the ground immediately each morning and walk in the direction we want to go in.

Everything I share, including this book, aims to boost your chances of success through real-world applications and insights. While no strategy guarantees 100% success, combining this content with your effort can guide you towards your goals.

Explore my website, www.retailleadersroadmap.com, and connect with me on social media. Dive into videos, interact with valuable content, or find resources that support your journey.

This book isn't just for reading from start to finish. Use it as a tool when you're stuck, whether you're struggling to achieve a personal goal or facing challenges with others. It can also be a thoughtful gift for team members or loved ones who are trying to find their way. Point them to sections that can address their specific hurdles.

I'm here to support you, your team, or your organization. Words have power, and I believe in using my experiences to resonate with you, your team, or your entire organization on a meaningful level.

Your character is the bedrock of your success, supporting everything else. Your relationships create the environment for effective leadership, and your strategy provides the framework to accomplish your goals.

Lastly, I started this final thought talking about how we wake up in the morning.

Let's end it by talking about how we put our heads down comfortably at night.

Our uniforms may be stained with dirt.

Our minds may be exhausted.

But the satisfaction of leaving everything on the field... that's the sweet reward for a day well lived.

ABOUT THE AUTHOR

Brian Librach's career in retail is a testament to his belief that success isn't solely the product of pedigree, but of perseverance and passion.

Brian's retail roots run deep, with a lineage of retailers and merchants stretching back to his father and grandfather. Starting his work life in the 7th grade at a local pizzeria, he quickly transitioned to apparel retail in White Plains, New York at 16. Known for his dynamic energy and distinctive look, he has consistently pushed the boundaries of what's expected in retail management.

Launching his career at the young age of 21, Brian quickly established himself as a District Manager, rising to become a Regional Director by 25. His trajectory continued upward, and by 35, he was a Director of Stores, later ascending to the role of VP of Stores for Urban Outfitters at 38, running operations in the US and Canada. Since then, he also served as VP of Stores and Operations at Pacific Sunwear, as well as most recently running stores internationally in Canada for Old Navy.

Now residing on the sunny West Coast of Florida with his wife Mell, son Jax, their Bullmastiff and Boxer pups, and two parrots, Dolly and Apollo, Brian continues to embody his passion for coaching, mentoring, and leading the next generation of retail stars with The Retail Leader's Roadmap.

WALK WITH ME. LET'S GET UP AND GO TOGETHER.

Made in the USA
Las Vegas, NV
11 March 2024

87020461R00142